G000294896

MICROSOFT OFFICE 2000 FOR WINDOWS® FOR DUMMIES®

Quick Reference

by Doug Lowe

revised by Bjoern-Erik Hartsfvang

IDG BOOKS WORLDWIDE

IDG Books Worldwide, Inc.
An International Data Group Company

Foster City, CA ✦ Chicago, IL ✦ Indianapolis, IN ✦ New York, NY

Microsoft® Office 2000 For Windows® For Dummies® Quick Reference

Published by
IDG Books Worldwide, Inc.
An International Data Group Company
919 E. Hillsdale Blvd.
Suite 400
Foster City, CA 94404
www.idgbooks.com (IDG Books Worldwide Web site)
www.dummies.com (Dummies Press Web site)

Library of Congress Catalog Card No.: 98-88795

ISBN: 0-7645-0453-3

Printed in the United States of America

10 9 8 7 6 5 4 3 2 1

1P/ST/QU/ZZ/IN

Distributed in the United States by IDG Books Worldwide, Inc.

Distributed by CDG Books Canada Inc. for Canada; by Transworld Publishers Limited in the United Kingdom; by IDG Norge Books for Norway; by IDG Sweden Books for Sweden; by Woodslane Pty. Ltd. for Australia; by Woodslane (NZ) Ltd. for New Zealand; by TransQuest Publishers Pte Ltd. for Singapore, Malaysia, Thailand, Indonesia, and Hong Kong; by ICG Muse, Inc. for Japan; by Norma Comunicaciones S.A. for Colombia; by Intersoft for South Africa; by Le Monde en Tique for France; by International Thomson Publishing for Germany, Austria and Switzerland; by Distribuidora Cuspide for Argentina; by Livraria Cultura for Brazil; by Ediciones ZETA S.C.R. Ltda. for Peru; by WS Computer Publishing Corporation, Inc., for the Philippines; by Contemporanea de Ediciones for Venezuela; by Express Computer Distributors for the Caribbean and West Indies; by Micronesia Media Distributor, Inc. for Micronesia; by Grupo Editorial Norma S.A. for Guatemala; by Chips Computadoras S.A. de C.V. for Mexico; by Editorial Norma de Panama S.A. for Panama; by American Bookshops for Finland. Authorized Sales Agent: Anthony Rudkin Associates for the Middle East and North Africa.

For general information on IDG Books Worldwide's books in the U.S., please call our Consumer Customer Service department at 800-762-2974. For reseller information, including discounts and premium sales, please call our Reseller Customer Service department at 800-434-3422.

For information on where to purchase IDG Books Worldwide's books outside the U.S., please contact our International Sales department at 317-596-5530 or fax 317-596-5692.

For consumer information on foreign language translations, please contact our Customer Service department at 1-800-434-3422, fax 317-596-5692, or e-mail rights@idgbooks.com.

For information on licensing foreign or domestic rights, please phone +1-650-655-3109.

For sales inquiries and special prices for bulk quantities, please contact our Sales department at 650-655-3200 or write to the address above.

For information on using IDG Books Worldwide's books in the classroom or for ordering examination copies, please contact our Educational Sales department at 800-434-2086 or fax 317-596-5499.

For press review copies, author interviews, or other publicity information, please contact our Public Relations department at 650-655-3000 or fax 650-655-3299.

For authorization to photocopy items for corporate, personal, or educational use, please contact Copyright Clearance Center, 222 Rosewood Drive, Danvers, MA 01923, or fax 978-750-4470.

is a registered trademark or trademark under exclusive license to IDG Books Worldwide, Inc. from International Data Group, Inc. in the United States and/or other countries.

About the Author

Doug Lowe has written more than 30 computer books, including IDG Books Worldwide's PowerPoint 97 For Windows For Dummies, Word 97 SECRETS, and Internet Explorer 3.0 For Dummies, and he know how to present boring technostuff in a style that is both entertaining and enlightening. He lives in sunny Fresno, California, with his wife Debbie, three adorable daughters, and two female golden retrievers, and he considers himself significantly outnumbered.

Acknowledgments

Thanks to Kel Oliver for keeping this book on track in spite of hectic schedules. And to Michael Lerch: Thanks for your technical contributions in making this book both readable and accurate.

ABOUT IDG BOOKS WORLDWIDE

Welcome to the world of IDG Books Worldwide.

IDG Books Worldwide, Inc., is a subsidiary of International Data Group, the world's largest publisher of computer-related information and the leading global provider of information services on information technology. IDG was founded more than 30 years ago by Patrick J. McGovern and now employs more than 9,000 people worldwide. IDG publishes more than 290 computer publications in over 75 countries. More than 90 million people read one or more IDG publications each month.

Launched in 1990, IDG Books Worldwide is today the #1 publisher of best-selling computer books in the United States. We are proud to have received eight awards from the Computer Press Association in recognition of editorial excellence and three from Computer Currents' First Annual Readers' Choice Awards. Our best-selling ...For Dummies® series has more than 50 million copies in print with translations in 31 languages. IDG Books Worldwide, through a joint venture with IDG's Hi-Tech Beijing, became the first U.S. publisher to publish a computer book in the People's Republic of China. In record time, IDG Books Worldwide has become the first choice for millions of readers around the world who want to learn how to better manage their businesses.

Our mission is simple: Every one of our books is designed to bring extra value and skill-building instructions to the reader. Our books are written by experts who understand and care about our readers. The knowledge base of our editorial staff comes from years of experience in publishing, education, and journalism — experience we use to produce books to carry us into the new millennium. In short, we care about books, so we attract the best people. We devote special attention to details such as audience, interior design, use of icons, and illustrations. And because we use an efficient process of authoring, editing, and desktop publishing our books electronically, we can spend more time ensuring superior content and less time on the technicalities of making books.

You can count on our commitment to deliver high-quality books at competitive prices on topics you want to read about. At IDG Books Worldwide, we continue in the IDG tradition of delivering quality for more than 30 years. You'll find no better book on a subject than one from IDG Books Worldwide.

John Kilcullen
Chairman and CEO
IDG Books Worldwide, Inc.

Steven Berkowitz
President and Publisher
IDG Books Worldwide, Inc.

Eighth Annual
Computer Press
Awards ≥1992

WINNER

Ninth Annual
Computer Press
Awards ≥1993

WINNER

Tenth Annual
Computer Press
Awards ≥1994

WINNER

Eleventh Annual
Computer Press
Awards ≥1995

Publisher's Acknowledgments

We're proud of this book; please register your comments through our IDG Books Worldwide Online Registration Form located at: http://my2cents.dummies.com.

Some of the people who helped bring this book to market include the following:

Acquisitions, Editorial, and Media Development

Project Editor: Kelly Oliver

Acquisitions Editor: Steve Hayes

(Previous Edition: Mary Goodwin)

Technical Editor: Michael Lerch

Editorial Manager: Mary Corder

Editorial Assistant: Paul Kuzmic

Production

Project Coordinator: E. Shawn Aylsworth

Layout and Graphics: Angela F. Hunckler, Brent Savage, M. Anne Sipahimalani, Drew Moore, Janet Seib, Tyler Connor, Mark Shirar, Brian Torwelle, Jacque Schneider

Proofreaders: Kelli Botta, Christine Berman

Indexer: Sherry Massey

Special Help

Suzanne Thomas

General and Administrative

IDG Books Worldwide, Inc.: John Kilcullen, CEO; Steven Berkowitz, President and Publisher

IDG Books Technology Publishing: Brenda McLaughlin, Senior Vice President and Group Publisher

Dummies Technology Press and Dummies Editorial: Diane Graves Steele, Vice President and Associate Publisher; Mary Bednarek, Director of Acquisitions and Product Development; Kristin A. Cocks, Editorial Director

Dummies Trade Press: Kathleen A. Welton, Vice President and Publisher; Kevin Thornton, Acquisitions Manager

IDG Books Production for Dummies Press: Michael R. Britton, Vice President of Production and Creative Services; Cindy L. Phipps, Manager of Project Coordination, Production Proofreading, and Indexing; Kathie S. Schutte, Supervisor of Page Layout; Shelley Lea, Supervisor of Graphics and Design; Debbie J. Gates, Production Systems Specialist; Robert Springer, Supervisor of Proofreading; Debbie Stailey, Special Projects Coordinator; Tony Augsburger, Supervisor of Reprints and Bluelines

Dummies Packaging and Book Design: Patty Page, Manager, Promotions Marketing

◆

The publisher would like to give special thanks to Patrick J. McGovern, without whom this book would not have been possible.

◆

Contents at a Glance

Table of Contents

How to Use This Book

Greetings! Welcome to *Microsoft Office 2000 For Windows For Dummies Quick Reference,* the Microsoft Office 2000 reference book that is recommended by three out of four computer gurus surveyed.

You have found the perfect book if you are one of the hapless souls who must use Microsoft Office 2000 but don't really want to become an expert in anything remotely related to computers. This book is a guiding star for those of you who still have a life outside of Office 2000 and don't want to spend hours figuring out how to do things that should be easy.

About This Book

This book does not teach you how to use Microsoft Office 2000 from the ground up. If you're a complete beginner when it comes to Office 2000, I suggest that you pick up a copy of Wally Wang and Roger Parker's *Microsoft Office 2000 For Windows For Dummies.* Or take a shopping cart through the computer book aisle at your local bookstore and get copies of *Word 2000 For Windows For Dummies* (Dan Gookin), *Excel 2000 For Windows For Dummies* (Greg Harvey), *PowerPoint 2000 For Windows For Dummies* (Yours Truly), *Microsoft Outlook For Dummies* (Bill Dyszel), and *Access 2000 For Windows For Dummies* (John Kaufeld), all from IDG Books Worldwide, Inc. These books tell you everything you need to know about using the programs that come with Office 2000.

This book is meant to be more of an "I forgot how to do that" book. It's for those embarrassing moments when you should know how to insert a chart, but you can't quite remember which command to use. Or when you want to quickly look up the keyboard shortcut that enables you to switch to Outline view. Or when you know that there's a quick way to do a Word 2000 mail merge using data stored in an Access 2000 database, but you're not quite sure what it is.

Turn to this book when you want 30-Second-Right-Now-Don't-Waste-My-Time answers to your questions. You don't find pages and pages of tireless prose exploring all the subtle nuances of each Office 2000 command. Instead, you get concise explanations of how to perform what I think are the most important and useful tasks and procedures.

How to Use This Book

Keep this book within arm's reach of your computer. Whenever you're about to do something you're not 100-percent sure about, grab this book before reaching for your mouse and look up what you're about to do to refresh your memory.

The best way to use this book is probably to use the index to find the procedure you're having trouble with and then turn to the indicated page to find out how to perform the procedure. Tasks that are common to all the programs — such as opening and closing files — are found in Part II. Procedures for performing complex tasks are found in Part IX. Tasks that are specific to the individual programs are found in the parts in between.

What Are All These Parts?

This book is divided into the following nine parts:

Part I: Getting to Know Microsoft Office 2000. This brief introduction to Microsoft Office 2000 explains what each Office 2000 program does.

Part II: Doing Common Chores. This part describes several features common to all the programs, such as opening and closing files, working with the Office Assistant, and so on.

Part III: Word 2000. This part contains reference information about Word 2000 for Windows, the ultimate word processing program. This part also summarizes the steps for common procedures that you perform in Word 2000.

Part IV: Excel 2000. This part covers Excel 2000, the last word in spreadsheet programs. You find information about the most common Excel 2000 functions and procedures here.

Part V: PowerPoint 2000. This part covers PowerPoint 2000, the desktop presentation program for creating slides, overhead transparencies, and on-screen slide shows. Once again, I provide information about the most common PowerPoint 2000 procedures.

Part VI: Access 2000. If you own the Professional Edition of Microsoft Office 2000, you'll appreciate this part, which covers this top-notch database program.

Part VII: Outlook 2000. Office 2000 comes with a new program called Outlook, which not only enables you to keep an up-to-date appointment and address book on your computer, but also handles all your e-mail. This part covers the most common procedures for Outlook 2000.

Part VIII: Publisher 2000. This part covers Publisher 2000, the desktop publishing program that allows you to create newsletters, pamphlets, posters, and much more. Again, I provide information about the most common procedures in Publisher 2000.

Part IX: Completing Complex Tasks. There are many tasks that you can perform in Office that are beyond the pale of most computer users, such as using OLE, hyperlinks, or writing macros. This part covers the most common tasks of this caliber of work.

What All the Pretty Pictures Mean

This book is strewn with little pictures designed to convey information quickly. Here's the lowdown on the icons you find in these pages:

Danger! Danger! You may be putting your files, your system, or yourself at risk if you don't heed these warnings.

This helpful information can save you time and effort.

This icon points out the quickest way to do something.

Watch it; something that's quirky or that doesn't work the way you think it should lurks near.

This icon points to a neat feature of Office 2000 and the programs that come with it or perhaps a helpful shortcut or insider tip.

This icon points out ways to use Microsoft's new IntelliMouse, which has that funky wheel-thing between the mouse buttons.

This icon indicates that you can find more information about a particular topic in another *...For Dummies* book.

Other Stuff You Should Know

On occasion, this book directs you to use keyboard shortcuts to get things done. Suppose that you see something like:

Ctrl+Z

It means to press and hold the Ctrl key as you press the Z key and then to release both keys together. You don't type the plus sign.

Sometimes I tell you to use a menu command, as follows:

File⇨Open

This line means to use the keyboard or mouse to open the File menu and then choose the Open command. The underlined letters are the keyboard hot keys for the command. You can use the hot keys first by pressing the Alt key. In the preceding example, you could press and release the Alt key, press and release the F key, and then press and release the O key.

Anything that I instruct you to type appears in bold, as follows: Type **b:setup** in the Run dialog box. Type the boldfaced text exactly as it appears; spaces between words *are* important.

Part I

Getting to Know Microsoft Office 2000

One thing's for sure: You get your money's worth with Microsoft Office 2000. In one convenient bundle, you get a world-class word processor, spreadsheet, presentation program, and database program. Plus, you get a grab bag full of other useful programs. What a bargain!

This part provides a general overview of the various pieces that make up Office 2000 so that you can get an idea of how the pieces fit together.

In this part . . .

✔ **What each of the major Office 2000 applications does**

Seeing What All Those Programs Do

The standard Microsoft Office 2000 package comes with four programs: Word 2000, Excel 2000, PowerPoint 2000, and Outlook 2000. The more expensive Microsoft Office 2000 Professional Edition comes with the same four programs plus a database program called Access 2000 and a desktop publishing program called Publisher 2000.

Word 2000

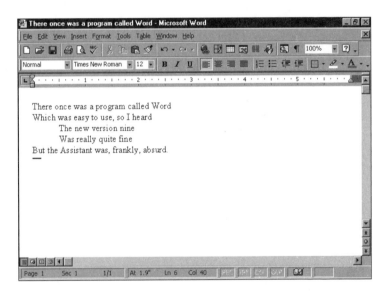

Microsoft Word 2000 for Windows (also called Word 9) is one of the best word-processing programs available. The program enables you to create documents of all shapes and sizes, from small letters and memos to medium-sized term papers and reports to humongous books and reports from Independent Prosecutors.

See also Part III of this book for more information about Word 2000.

Excel 2000

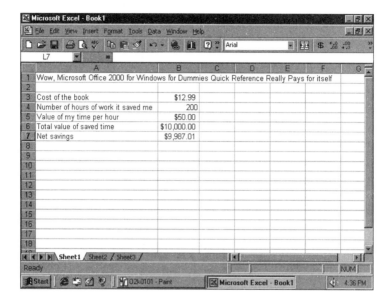

Excel 2000, also known as Excel 9, is a spreadsheet program. It's the bean-counter of the Office 2000 operation. Excel 2000 excels at adding up budget totals, calculating sales commissions, figuring loan payments, and performing other math-oriented chores. Just like other spreadsheet programs, Excel 2000 presents its data as a large table that consists of rows and columns. The intersection of a row and column is called a *cell*. You can use cells to store text, numbers, or formulas that calculate results based on the contents of other cells.

See also Part IV of this book.

PowerPoint 2000

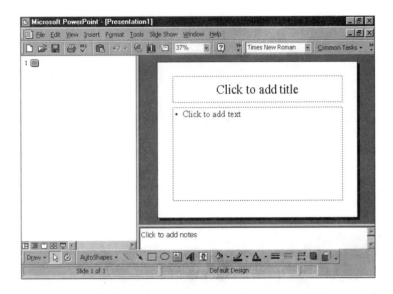

PowerPoint 2000 (also sometimes known as PowerPoint 9) is the oddball program of the Office 2000 suite. Many people buy Office 2000 because they need a word processor and a spreadsheet program, and buying the standard Office 2000 package is cheaper than buying Word 2000 and Excel 2000 separately. So the rest of what comes with Office 2000 is basically free. And that includes PowerPoint 2000.

So what the heck is PowerPoint 2000? It's a desktop presentation program, which means that the program is designed to help you make presentations. You can use PowerPoint 2000 whether you're speaking in front of hundreds of people at a shareholders' meeting, to a group of sales reps at a sales conference, or with a client one-on-one at a restaurant.

If you work with overhead transparencies or 35mm slides, PowerPoint 2000 is just the program you need. PowerPoint 2000 can create slides in any of several formats and can also create handouts for your audience as well as notes for you so that you don't get lost in the middle of your speech.

You can also use PowerPoint 2000 to create files that you can publish on the World Wide Web.

See also Part V of this book for reference information about PowerPoint 2000.

Access 2000

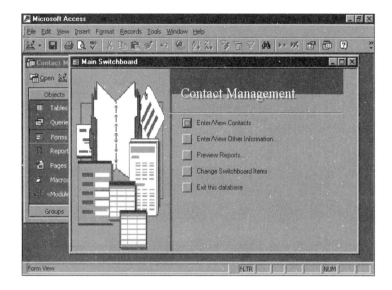

Access 2000, a database program, is the computer equivalent of
the shoe box in which you store your tax records. Access 2000 is
better than the shoe box in many ways, because Access keeps
your records in order, enables you to print reports that list and
summarize your data in any form imaginable, and doesn't crumple
your papers. On the negative side, Access 2000 is a lot harder to
use than your average shoe box.

Access 2000 (also known as Access 9) comes with the more
expensive packages of Microsoft Office 2000 (Professional,
Premium, and Developer); the program isn't in the bargain-
basement, standard Office 2000 package.

Of the programs that come with Office 2000, Access 2000 is the
hardest one to conquer, but learning it may be the most worth-
while. Database programs, such as Access 2000, are well suited for
keeping mailing lists, but if a mailing list is the only reason you
need Access 2000, don't bother. Word 2000 does a pretty good job
of storing mailing lists all by itself. If, however, you want to keep an
inventory of your CDs or books, or if you want to keep a record of
sales orders or employee performance, Access is unbeatable.

You can also use Access 2000 to set up databases that you can
access from the World Wide Web.

See also Part VI of this book for more information about
Access 2000.

Outlook 2000

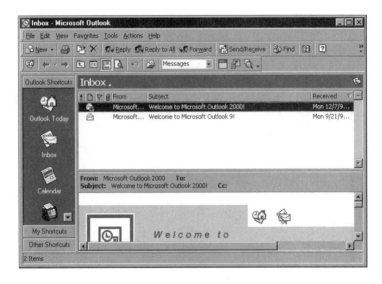

Outlook 2000 is the computer equivalent of one of those fancy combination appointment book/address books — a time-management program that enables you to schedule appointments, create a To Do list, and keep track of your important contacts. But more than that, Outlook 2000 is also an all-in-one e-mail program from which you can send and receive electronic mail over the Internet, your office network, or any of several popular online services.

See also Part VII of this book for more information about Outlook 2000.

Publisher 2000

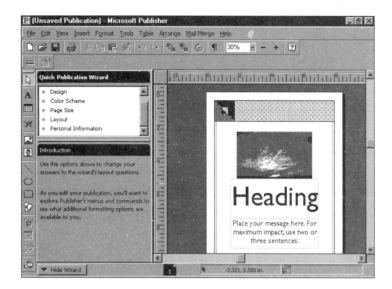

Publisher 2000 is the Microsoft desktop publishing program, and it's available in the Office 2000 Premium Edition. You can use Publisher to create professional-looking documents suitable for publication. Publisher can create everything from single-page leaflets to posters to newsletters with full-color photographs.

Publisher provides you with document templates to cover nearly every imaginable type of document you want to create, and then it allows you to customize your document so that you can create your own personal look and feel.

See also Part VIII of this book for more information about Publisher 2000.

Part II

Doing Common Chores

In this part, you find out how to work with tasks that are fairly common among the different Office programs. Some of these are fairly basic; others are more advanced. What they all have in common is that you can be sure that they work mostly the same way in the different programs of the Office 2000 suite.

In this part . . .

- ✓ Using the Clipboard to cut, copy, and paste
- ✓ Opening and closing documents
- ✓ Creating new documents and retrieving existing documents from disk
- ✓ Copying documents
- ✓ Deleting documents
- ✓ Printing your documents
- ✓ Making your documents ready for the World Wide Web
- ✓ Opening, exiting, and switching your Office programs
- ✓ Saving documents to disk
- ✓ Using Help
- ✓ Using the spell checker
- ✓ Using the new mouse with the wheel thingy

Clipboard

The *Clipboard* is the program that enables you to move data within a file, between files, or between programs, and it has been a standard part of all Windows programs since the first version of Windows. The following sections describe how to copy and move data by using the Clipboard.

Copying data

You can make a copy of a selection of a document and put that copy somewhere else. The procedure for copying data is the same whether the new location for the copied data is in the same document, is in a different document using the same program (such as copying from a Word document to a Word document), or is in a different program (such as copying from Word to Excel). To make a duplicate copy of text, follow these steps:

1. Select the text you want to copy.

The easiest way to select text is to position your cursor at the beginning of the selection and press the left mouse button. Continue to hold down the mouse button and drag the mouse so that you highlight all the text you want to select. Release the mouse button and the text is selected. This procedure can also be used to select entire cells in Excel.

2. Choose Edit⇨Copy, press Ctrl+C, or click the Copy button on the Standard toolbar.

The Standard toolbar is the toolbar that appears by default along the top of your application window. If you don't see a toolbar that you wish to use, click View⇨Toolbars. This will show you a list of all the available toolbars for that application.

3. Move the cursor to the location where you want to insert the text.

4. Choose Edit⇨Paste, press Ctrl+V, or click the Paste button on the Standard toolbar.

Dragging and dropping text

You can move text from one location to another by using the drag-and-drop technique. This works only when you're moving text or pictures within the same document.

Before using this feature, you must make sure that the drag-and-drop option is enabled. To do this, select Tools⇨Options. When the Options dialog box appears, click the Edit tab and make sure that the drag-and-drop feature is checked. (The name of the drag-and-drop feature varies between programs; for example, in Word it's called Drag-and-Drop Text Editing, but in Excel it's called Allow Cell Drag and Drop.)

When drag-and-drop is enabled, you can use it as follows:

1. Select the text that you want to move.

2. Place the mouse pointer anywhere over the selected text and then press and hold the left mouse button.

3. Drag the text to the location where you want to move the text.

4. Release the mouse button.

To copy rather than move text, press and hold the Ctrl key while dragging the text.

Moving data

The procedure for moving data is basically the same within all the applications of Office 2000, whether you're moving data within the same document, between two documents running on the same program, or between two documents running on different programs (such as moving an Excel spreadsheet to a Word document). To do this:

1. Open the program and the file that contains the data that you want to move.

If the program isn't already running, start it by choosing it from the Start⇨Programs menu.

2. Select the data that you want to move by using the mouse or keyboard.

 3. Press Ctrl+X, choose Edit⇨Cut, or click the Cut button, which appears on the Standard toolbar of all the Office 2000 programs.

4. Position the cursor where you want to insert the data.

If you're putting the selection in another document, you have to open that document first.

 5. Press Ctrl+V, choose Edit⇨Paste, or click the Paste button, which appears on the Standard toolbar of all the Office 2000 programs.

One of the really neat things about Office 2000 is that most of the time it automatically formats information that you transfer between programs to work within the new program. (Sometimes you have to help Office with the formatting, and sometimes you don't.) Thus a spreadsheet in Excel (or a series of records from

Access) are magically turned into a table when you move them to Word. However, If you're moving data from Word to Excel, you need to organize the data into columns by using the Tab key to divide the different categories of information. Information from Access is pasted into Excel with each record as a separate row and the fields organized by column. Now, if you want to paste something that Office can't format to fit the new program (such as moving a few paragraphs of a Word document into an Excel spreadsheet), it inserts the data as an *embedded object*. If you double-click the embedded object, the program that contains the embedded object opens the original program with the data you transferred. You can look at the information or modify it as you see fit from this point on, and the changes will remain in the embedded object; the next time you double-click the embedded object, you'll see the change. If Office simply cannot work with the information or the program that you've moved into another program, it inserts a picture of the program. This isn't an embedded object; you can't do anything with it except delete it.

Closing a File

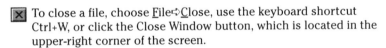 To close a file, choose File➪Close, use the keyboard shortcut Ctrl+W, or click the Close Window button, which is located in the upper-right corner of the screen.

 When you look at the upper-right corner of the screen, you see two Close buttons. The top button of the two (the one next to the other two buttons) closes the *program;* the Close Window button just below it closes the *file*. If you don't want to close the program you've been working in, make sure that you click the Close Window button.

 You don't need to close files before exiting a program. If you exit the program without closing a file, the program closes the file for you. But closing files you're no longer working with is a good idea because doing so saves memory, which may, in turn, help your programs run faster.

If you close a file and have made changes to the file since you last saved it, a dialog box appears, offering to save the changes for you. Click the Yes button to save the file before closing or click the No button to abandon any changes you made to the file.

 If you have only one file open and you close that file, you may discover that you've inadvertently rendered most of the program's commands inaccessible — they appear "grayed out" on the menus, and clicking them does nothing. Don't panic. Open another file or create a new file, and the commands return to life.

Creating a Document

You have several ways to create a new document in Word 2000, Excel 2000, Access 2000, or PowerPoint 2000:

✦ **Choose File⇨New.** This command summons the New dialog box, which enables you to select one of several available templates you want to use as the basis of your new document. All four of the major programs in Office 2000 provide templates for the most common types of documents created in these programs.

 ✦ **Click the New button in the Standard toolbar.** Clicking the New button bypasses the New dialog box and creates an empty new document.

✦ **Press Ctrl+N.** This keyboard shortcut creates an empty new document as well.

 You can't create an empty new document in Access. Regardless of how you tell your system you want to make a new Access document, you always see the New dialog box, which gives you a list of templates and options to work with. You can, however, click the Database icon on the General tab of this dialog box. Clicking Database opens an empty database document that you can format and play with to your heart's content.

E-Mail

 If your computer is connected to a network or to the Internet, you can send a copy of the file you're working on to a friend or co-worker via e-mail by following these steps:

1. Choose File⇨Send To⇨Mail Recipient (as Attachment).

If the program asks you to specify a user profile, select the profile you normally use in sending and receiving e-mail. User profiles control such things as which e-mail services you have access to and where your address book is stored. If more than one person uses your computer, you can set up a separate profile for each user. If possible, talk to the person responsible for setting up your e-mail system about configuring your user profile for you.

2. You can type someone's e-mail address in the To text box. Or you can click the To button to summon your address book, which should contain the e-mail addresses of the people you routinely correspond with.

3. Select the recipient from your address book and then click the OK button in the Address Book dialog box.

4. Click the <u>S</u>end button to send the message.

Exiting Programs

Had enough excitement for one day? Use any one of the following techniques to shut down your program:

✦ Choose <u>F</u>ile⇨E<u>x</u>it.

 ✦ Click the Close button that appears at the upper-right corner of the program window. The Close button is marked by an X, proving the old adage that X does, indeed, mark the spot.

✦ Press Alt+F4.

You can't abandon ship until you save your work. If you made changes to any files and haven't saved them, a dialog box asks whether you want to save your files. Tell it Yes.

Never just turn off your computer while a program is running. This can damage your computer and can leave file fragments cluttering up your hard drive. Always exit all programs that are running *before* you turn off your computer. In fact, you should always notify Windows before you turn off your computer by clicking the Start button and then choosing the Shut Down command. This summons a Shut Down dialog box. To shut down your computer, click the Yes button.

Help

Lost within the dark woods of Office 2000 and don't know how to get out? Fret not, for all the Office 2000 programs boast an excellent Help system that can answer all your questions — provided, of course, that you know what your questions are.

The following list summarizes the more notable methods of getting help:

✦ The universal Help key is F1. Press F1 at any time, and the Office Assistant rushes to your aid. If you have turned the Office Assistant off, then a Help window opens instead.

✦ If you have not turned off the Office Assistant and you press F1 while you're in the middle of something, the Office Assistant tries to figure out what you're doing so it can give you help tailored for that task. This slick little bit of wizardry is called *context-sensitive Help*.

✦ After you click Help in the menu bar, you get an entire menu of Help stuff, most of which is only moderately helpful. Choosing Help➪Help either summons the Office Assistant or opens the Help window.

✦ You can also call up Help in just about any dialog box by clicking the question mark button that appears in the top-right corner of the dialog box. The mouse pointer changes to an arrow with a question mark grafted onto its back. You can then click anything in the dialog box to get specific information about that feature.

 ✦ You can also click the Office Assistant button on the Standard toolbar — the toolbar that sits just beneath the menu bar — to summon the Office Assistant.

 ✦ For a really cool kind of help, try choosing Help➪What's This? This Help feature changes the mouse pointer into a pointy question mark, with which you can click just about anything on-screen in order to get an explanation of the object that you click.

Detect and Repair

Like everything else in our lives, computer programs can suffer wear-and-tear from regular use. Eventually our applications can become tattered and ragged, which can result in crashed programs and lost or garbled data. If this had happened in the bad old days, the only thing you could have done would have been to erase the program from your system and reinstall it, an annoying and time-consuming task and one that would have lost any customized settings that you had made on your system. But no more! We now have the Detect and Repair feature as part of the Help menu.

Detect and Repair is actually a feature of Windows 98, so if you're running Office 2000 on Windows 95, you're out of luck. But for the rest of us (especially overworked authors who beat the dickens out of their Word programs on a daily basis), Detect and Repair can be a godsend. This wonderful little tool scans your application for damage and fixes it for you in a fraction of the time that it would have taken to delete and install the application again. And it has a feature that allows you to retain your customized settings.

To use the Detect and Repair feature:

1. Open the Office program that you need to repair.

2. Select Help➪Detect and Repair.

The Detect and Repair dialog box opens.

3. Make sure that a check mark appears in the Restore My Shortcuts While Repairing check box.

Selecting this option saves your customization.

4. Click the Start button.

After you set the process in motion, your system thinks about things for a few moments and then asks you to insert the Office installation disk.

5. Insert the Office installation disk and click OK.

At this point, Windows starts analyzing the application. Depending on the speed of your system, this could take a few minutes, so go get a snack while you're waiting for it to do its thing.

When the self-diagnostic is finished, you see a dialog box that tells you that you must restart your computer for the changes to take effect.

6. Either click Yes to restart immediately (which is what I would recommend) or click No and do it yourself later.

Help the old-fashioned way

When I was a kid, I didn't have fancy Office Assistants to bail me out if I needed help. No sir. I had to walk three miles through the snow in bare feet to get my help. That's why, in the old days, I appreciated all the help I could get.

If you yearn for the good old days, back when you actually had to *search* for Help topics, you can always revert to Windows-style Help. Here's how to search for Help on a specific topic the old-fashioned way:

1. Before you can open the Help window, you first must turn the Office Assistant off. Do this by right-clicking the Office Assistant, clicking Options from the drop-down menu, and removing the check from the Use the Office Assistant check box. Then click OK.

2. Choose Help➪Help, or press F1.

Notice that the actual name of the item on the Help drop-down menu depends on the application you're using. If you are asking for help in Word, the menu says Microsoft Word Help. If you're using PowerPoint, the menu says Microsoft PowerPoint Help. Don't worry; they're all essentially the same.

The Help Topics window appears, as shown here for Word 2000.

The left side of the Help window has three tabs: Contents, Answer Wizard, and Index. Each one of the tabs allows you to find the same information through a different route.

- The Answer Wizard works like the Office Assistant. The What Would You Like to Do? text box allows you to ask a question or a topic. Type in the task you want to learn about (say you want to add a border) and click the Search button. The information appears in the right-hand window.

- When you first look at the Contents tab, it appears to organize the helpful information by topic, like the chapters of a book. Click the plus sign to the left of the topic (for example: Borders, Lines, and Shading), and the topic expands to show you a list of tasks associated with that topic. Click the task you want to learn (such as Add a Border) and the window on the right of the window shows you either the information you requested or gives you a list of specific tasks. If you see the list of specific tasks, click the one you need information about, and you (finally!) get to the directions to complete the task. Generally, the more complex the task, the more levels of the Contents directory you have to go through to get to the information.

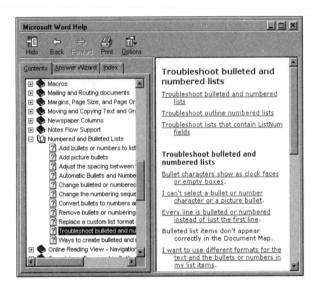

In the figure showing the Contents tab, bulleted lists are shown under the heading Numbered and Bulleted Lists. The great weakness of the Contents tab is that you have to guess how Microsoft organized the information, and you don't have the option of typing a query. However, if you type the query either in the Index or the Answer Wizard tab and then click the Contents tab, the corresponding information appears there as well.

• If the Contents tab is like the table of contents in the front of a book, then the Index tab is just like the index in the back of the same book. There are two ways to use this tab. You can enter a keyword (such as border) into the Type Keywords text box, or you can scroll through the Or Choose Keywords list box until you find what you're looking for. After you've typed the keyword or found it in the list, click the Search button. You get a list of topics in the Choose a Topic window, located at the bottom of the Index tab. This window includes the number of topics associated with the keyword (FYI, borders has 47 topics). Scroll through this list until you find the specific topic you want and double-click it. As with the other tabs, the information you want then appears on the right side of the Help window.

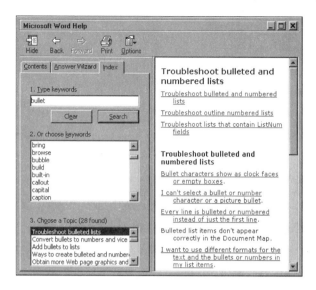

3. When you are done looking up the information, click the Close button in the upper right-hand corner of the Help window and get back to work.

Help on the Internet

You can also get help directly from Microsoft via the World Wide Web, assuming that you have access to the Internet from your computer. The Help menu includes a Microsoft on the Web command that features links to various Web sites that provide information about Microsoft Office products. Your best bet for online Help is to choose Help⇨Office on the Web. This command launches the Internet Explorer Web browser to display the Microsoft online support page for the program you're using.

From this page, you can access useful articles about specific topics of interest. Plus, you can access a list of frequently asked questions or the Microsoft Knowledge Base, a huge searchable database that contains answers to thousands of technical questions.

But the most valuable link on the online support page is the Visit Our Newsgroups link. Click this link to enter the Microsoft product support newsgroups, where you can leave a detailed question that should be answered within a few days.

Office Assistant

The Office Assistant is a friendly little helper that lives on your screen, eager to help you out any time you need or want it. The Assistant watches you work and periodically chimes in with a tip about how you could perform a task more efficiently. And the Assistant is always there, either visible on-screen or lurking behind the scene waiting for your summons.

If the Office Assistant is nowhere to be found, you can summon it quickly by clicking the Office Assistant button on the Standard toolbar. To ask a question, click the Office Assistant. A balloon dialog box appears, as shown in the following example:

Tell the Assistant what you want to do by typing a few keywords in the balloon's text box (for example, you could type **create a bullet list** or even just **bullet list**) and then click the Search button. The Assistant thinks for a moment and then shows you a list of Help topics related to your keywords. Click the topic you're interested in to display the Help.

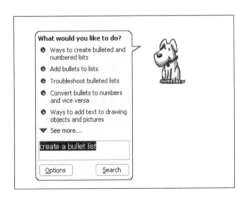

If you don't like Rocky, the cute little puppy that is your default Office Assistant, you can change it to one of nine different Assistants: the Genius, a Smiley Face, Mother Nature, a robot, the Office logo, or several other choices. To change the Assistant's character, right-click the Office Assistant and select Choose Assistant from the dialog box that appears. Use the Back and Next buttons on the dialog box to look at the available choices. When you find the one you like best, make sure that it's visible in the dialog box and click OK. It appears on your screen.

You can customize your Office Assistant to behave in ways that are most appealing or useful to you. To do this, click the Options button in the Office Assistant's dialog box (or right-click the Office Assistant and select Options from that dialog box). The Options tab of the Office Assistant dialog box appears. You can use the check boxes on this dialog box to specify exactly how you want your Office Assistant to work for you, up to and including turning the Office Assistant off. How you customize your Office Assistant is up to you; you may want to try experimenting with different features turned on and off until you find the settings that work best for you and your needs. When you have the settings the way you want them, click OK and go back to work.

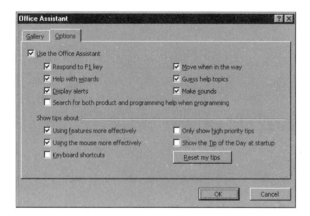

IntelliMouse

If you have the new Microsoft IntelliMouse, you can use its wheel control to scroll through your document. Just roll the wheel to scroll forward and back or click the wheel to switch to "pan" mode, which enables you to scroll through your document by dragging the mouse up or down. Click the wheel again to quit pan mode. You can also zoom in and out by pressing and holding the Ctrl key as you roll the wheel on the IntelliMouse.

Older Versions of Office

When Office 97 came out, many of us were dismayed to discover that our friends and co-workers who were using older versions of the software could not read the files we sent them. We could read theirs, but their systems couldn't handle the new formatting in the Office 97 Suite.

Fortunately, the files created by Office 2000 are readable by anyone using an Office 97 application. Unfortunately, anyone using Office 95 or older still can't translate the formatting of Office 2000.

Therefore, if you need to give files to an associate who is still in the dark ages of Office 95 (or — shudder — an even older version), you need to format your files so that they can be read. You can easily do this, but it means that you either have to change the formatting of your original file or create a new, duplicate file with the older formatting. To change the formatting of a document to be read by other programs:

1. Make sure that the document you want to reformat is open and currently saved.

2. Select File⇨Save As.

The Save As dialog box opens.

3. At the bottom of the dialog box is a Save as Type list box. Click the arrow to the right of the box to see the available file formatting options.

4. Scroll through the list to find the formatting that you need. Click your selection.

5. Make any other changes you want to save the document in the correct folder and with the right filename.

6. When you are finished, click the Open button in the lower right corner.

 If the person you are sending this file to is running a version of Office that is older than Office 95 or is not using a Microsoft product, make sure that the new filename that you're sending them does not include any spaces and has eight or fewer characters.

Opening a File

After you save your file to disk, you may want to retrieve the file later to make changes to it or to print it. Unless you've used it recently, you must first get to the Open dialog box before opening a file. This can be done in at least four ways:

+ Click the Open button on the Standard toolbar.

+ Choose File⇨Open.

+ Press Ctrl+O.

+ Press Ctrl+F12.

 If you have used the file recently, chances are that you can find it without using the Open dialog box (or even having the application running). To find the file quickly, click the Start button and select Documents. You get a list of the last fifteen documents that you have opened. If what you need is there, simply click the document name. The document and its application open for you.

If the Open dialog box shows the document folder where the file you want is located, simply click the file you want and then click the Open button or press Enter. If your file isn't listed as a choice, use the Look In drop-down list to rummage about your disk until you find the file.

The fastest way to open a file from inside the Open dialog box is to double-click the name of the file you want to open. Doing so spares you from first clicking the filename and then clicking the Open button. That's a phenomenally huge time saver.

Other controls on the Open dialog box are listed in the following table.

Control	What It Does
←	Moves you back to the last location that the Open window showed. If you hold your cursor over this button, a pop-up window appears to tell you what that last location is.
⬆	Moves you up one level in your computer's directory.
🔍	Opens the Internet Explorer to allow you to search the World Wide Web, which is useful if you're looking for a Web page.
✕	Deletes the highlighted document or folder. This is a new addition to Office 2000, and it means that you no longer have to open the Windows Explorer to get rid of files.
📁	Creates a new folder in the current location of the Open dialog box.
▦	The function of this button varies by what is currently shown in the dialog box. If only the icons and filenames are showing (called the List view), one click provides you with information about the size of all the files, the type of file, and the date they were modified (this is called the Details view). If you select one particular file and click this button again, the dialog box shows you a split screen. A window appears on the right with more information than you probably would ever want about that file (though some of it is quite useful). This is called the Properties view. Click the button a third time to see a small picture of the document (this is called a Preview). The Preview is handy if you want to know what the document says without opening it all the way. Click the button again, and you're back to seeing just the icons and filenames.
▦ ▾	If you click the arrow to the right of this button, you get a drop-down list of the different possible ways of displaying the documents and files of your system. In fact, these are the same views that you saw by clicking the main button (rather than the arrow) repeatedly (see the previous entry in this table). However, one other feature, Arrange Icons, allows you to organize how your files appear in the dialog box.
Tools ▾	This is actually a menu button. Clicking it gives you a drop-down list of commands, including Find, Delete, Rename, Print, Add to Favorites, Map Network Drive, and Properties.

Control	What It Does
History	Shows you a list of the documents that you have recently had open, regardless of their location.
My Documents	Shows the contents of the My Documents folder.
Desktop	Shows the contents of your desktop, including any shortcuts you've placed there.
Favorites	Displays your Favorites folder.
Web Folders	Displays any Web folders that you've saved to your system.

All the Office 2000 programs keep track of the last few files you opened and display the names of those files at the bottom of the File menu. To reopen a file that you opened recently, click the File menu and inspect the list of files at the bottom of the menu. If the filename you want appears in this list, click the filename to open that file.

 If you've looked through a folder and don't see a file that you *know* has to be there, click the Files of Type list box. The Open window displays only the types of files indicated in this box, so if Files of Type is set to show only Word files, you could have a dozen Excel files in the folder and not see them. If this happens, scroll to the type of file you want (or to the All Files selection), and click it. The correct file formats appear.

Printing a File

Follow this procedure to print your masterpiece:

1. Make sure that your printer is turned on and ready to print.

2. Open the Print dialog box by choosing File➪Print or by pressing Ctrl+P.

The Print dialog box enables you to print a single page or range of pages and to print more than one copy of the document. It also enables you to change the paper size and orientation and to select the printer you want to use.

 To print a single copy of your document quickly, without fussing with the Print dialog box, click the Print button in the Standard toolbar. One copy of your document appears on the printer.

Saving a File as a Web Document

Web documents are saved in what is called *HTML* format. HTML is a computer language that you use to format material for the Internet's World Wide Web. All the Office 2000 applications can easily save documents in the HTML format so you can display them on the Web.

To save a Word, Excel, or PowerPoint document as a Web page, all you need to do is choose File⇨Save as Web Page. This command opens the Save As dialog box, specifically set to save the file as a Web page. Simply find the folder where you want to store the file and click the Save button. The file can then be uploaded to your server at a later date.

Saving a Web page document in Access isn't quite as simple, but it's still easier than in the old days. To do save an Access document in HTML:

1. Make sure that the Access document you want to convert to HTML is open and on your screen.

2. Select File⇨Export.

3. In the Export dialog box, click the arrow to the right of the Save as Type list box (located at the bottom of the dialog box).

4. Scroll through the list until you see HTML Documents. Click that selection so that it appears in the list box.

5. As always, find the folder in which you want to save the file.

6. Click the Save button.

When you click the Save button, you see an HTML Output Options dialog box. This is an added feature that allows you to choose a template for your HTML document. Working with this feature is beyond the scope of this book, but you can select either a template supplied by Office or a template that you've added to your system. However, if you click OK with the HTML Template text box blank, your file will be saved as an HTML document without a specialized template.

Saving a File under a New Name

If you want to make a duplicate of the current file by saving the file under a different filename, follow these steps:

1. Choose File⇨Save As.

The Save As dialog box appears.

2. Use the Save In drop-down list to rummage about until you find the folder in which you want to save the file. Click the

Create Folder button if you want to create a new folder instead of using an existing one.

3. Type a new name for the file in the File Name text box.

4. Click the Save button.

Shortcuts That Work Everywhere

The following tables list keyboard shortcuts and toolbar buttons that work in all (or at least most of) the Office 2000 programs.

Editing commands

Toolbar button	Keyboard Shortcut	Equivalent Command
	Ctrl+X	Edit⇨Cut
	Ctrl+C	Edit⇨Copy
	Ctrl+V	Edit⇨Paste
	Ctrl+Z	Edit⇨Undo
	Ctrl+Y	Edit⇨Redo
	Ctrl+A	Edit⇨Select All
	Ctrl+F	Edit⇨Find
	Ctrl+H	Edit⇨Replace

File commands

Toolbar button	Keyboard Shortcut	Equivalent Command
	Ctrl+N	File⇨New
	Ctrl+O or Ctrl+F12	File⇨Open
	Ctrl+S	File⇨Save
	F12	File⇨Save As
	Ctrl+W	File⇨Close
	Ctrl+P	File⇨Print
	Alt+F4	File⇨Exit

Quick formatting

Toolbar button	Keyboard Shortcut	Format Applied
B	Ctrl+B	Bold
I	Ctrl+I	Italic
<u>U</u>	Ctrl+U	Underline
	Ctrl+spacebar	Return to normal format

Switching programs

Keyboard Shortcut	What It Does
Alt+Esc	Switches to the next program in line.
Alt+Tab	Displays the name of the next program in line. While holding the Alt key, press Tab to summon a list of icons for all the programs that are currently running. Keep pressing the Tab key until the icon for the program you want to switch to is highlighted, and then release both keys to switch to that program.
Ctrl+Esc	Pops up the taskbar and the Start menu. Click the button on the taskbar for the program you want to switch to.

Spell Checking

Office 2000 is designed so that you can check your spelling in any of its applications. You can check your spelling in two ways, depending on which program you're using. First, if you are using either Word or PowerPoint, the program can check your spelling as you type, highlighting misspelled words so that you can immediately correct them. Second, all the Office 2000 programs can check your spelling after you have typed your document, enabling you to forget about spelling as you write, with the knowledge that you can correct any mistakes later on.

Spell checking as you type

Unless you disabled the Office as-you-type spell checker, Word 2000 and PowerPoint 2000 spell check your words as you type. The program underlines any misspelled words with a wavy red line. To correct a misspelled word, click the word with the right mouse button. Then pick the correct spelling from the pop-up menu that appears.

If you don't like this automatic spell checking, you can disable the feature in either Word or PowerPoint by following these steps:

1. Choose Tools⇨Options to open the Options dialog box.

2. In Word, click the Spelling and Grammar tab. In PowerPoint, click the Spelling and Style tab.

3. Click the Check Spelling as You Type check box to deselect this option.

4. Click the OK button.

If you want to turn the automatic spell checker back on, just repeat the procedure, clicking the Check Spelling as You Type option to select it.

Spell checking after you type

If you disable the on-the-fly spell checking in Word and PowerPoint, you can always spell check your work after the fact. And you can spell check this way in all the Office 2000 programs. Here's how:

1. Choose Tools⇨Spelling (in Word, the command is Tools⇨ Spelling and Grammar), press F7, or click the Spelling button in the Standard toolbar.

Whichever method you choose, Office 2000 begins checking your spelling from the current cursor position. If the spell checker finds a misspelled word, the Spelling dialog box appears.

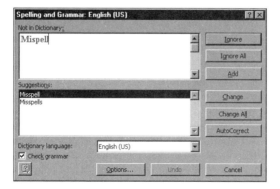

2. Depending on whether the word is misspelled, take one of the following actions:

- If the word really is misspelled, select the correct spelling from the list of suggested spellings that appears in the dialog box and click the Change button.

- If the correct spelling doesn't appear among the suggestions, type the correct spelling in the Not in Dictionary box and click the Change button.

- If the word is correctly spelled, click the Ignore button. Or click the Ignore All button to ignore any subsequent occurrences of the word.

3. Repeat Step 2 until the spell checker gives up.

After Office 2000 finishes with your spelling, a message appears to tell you it's done.

Starting Programs

To start an Office 2000 program, follow these steps:

1. Turn on your computer.

With luck, you need to flip or press only one switch to do so. But if your computer, monitor, and printer are plugged in separately, you must turn on each one separately. It takes a moment for your operating system (whether Windows 95 or Windows 98) to come to life; be patient.

2. Click the Start button.

Normally, the Start button is located at the bottom-left of the screen in the taskbar, but you can move the taskbar to any edge of the screen you want. If the Start button isn't visible anywhere on-screen, try moving the mouse all the way to the bottom edge of the screen to see whether the Start button appears. If that doesn't work, point to top, left, and right edges of the screen until the Start button appears.

After you click the Start button, the Start menu pops up.

3. Point to Programs in the Start menu.

4. Locate and click the program you want to start from the menu that appears.

You can place a shortcut for the programs you use most frequently either on the top level of the Start menu or on your desktop. To do this quickly and easily, open the Start menu and locate the program you want to make a shortcut for, click and hold the left mouse button on it, and drag it to where you want it. (If you want it on the top of the Start menu, drag it to the area of the Start menu over Programs; if you want it on the desktop, drag it there.) Then, whenever you want to open that program, simply click that icon.

Switching among Programs

Windows 95 and Windows 98 both allow you to run several programs at the same time and switch back and forth among those programs. By using this feature, for example, you can start up Word 2000, PowerPoint 2000, and Excel 2000 at the same time and quickly switch to any of the three programs to access or exchange information among them.

After you have more than one program running, you can switch among them by using any of the following techniques:

✦ **Press Alt+Esc:** You can switch to the next program in line by pressing Alt+Esc. If more than two programs are running, you may need to press this key combination several times to get to the program you want.

You can reverse the order in which Windows switches to programs by pressing Alt+Shift+Esc instead.

✦ **Press Alt+Tab:** Alt+Tab displays a menu of icons, representing all the programs currently running, in a window that appears in the middle of the screen. To switch to a program, hold down the Alt key and press the Tab key repeatedly until you select the program you want to use. Then release both keys to switch to that program.

✦ **Use the taskbar:** You can switch among programs easily by using the taskbar. Just click the button in the taskbar that represents the program to which you want to switch — and you're there!

The taskbar usually sits at the bottom of the screen, but you can also configure the taskbar to rest on any edge of the screen. You can even configure the taskbar so that the feature vanishes entirely if not in use. In that case, you must move the mouse pointer to the extreme bottom edge of the screen (or the left, right, or top edge, if you moved the taskbar) to access the feature again. If all else fails, you can locate the taskbar by pressing Ctrl+Esc, which reveals the taskbar no matter where it is. (Pressing Ctrl+Esc also opens the Start menu as if you had clicked the Start button.) After you locate the taskbar, you can then switch to any other running program by clicking that program's button on the taskbar.

Web Toolbar

In the old days of Office 97, the Web toolbar was only available in Word. Office 2000 gives you this feature in each of the four major programs of the suite. This toolbar enables you to browse Office documents that are linked together with hyperlinks more easily and to browse the Internet's World Wide Web. The Web toolbar is shown in the following figure:

Choose View⇨Toolbars to access the Web toolbar and to open the Toolbars drop-down list. Click the Web option, and the Web tool-bar appears on your screen. It stays there until you remove it by removing the check next to it on the View⇨Toolbars drop-down list.

At the far right of the Web toolbar is a list box in which you can type the filename of a file you want to open or the URL of an Internet address you would like to visit. The following table describes the other buttons in the Web toolbar:

Button	What It Does
⇦	Displays the previous page.
⇨	Displays the next page in sequence.
⊗	Cancels a download in process.
🔃	Obtains a new copy of the document or HTML page and refreshes your screen.
🏠	Takes you to your start page, which you designated in Internet Explorer 5.0 as the first page to display after you enter the Internet.
🔍	Calls up a search page that enables you to search the Internet for specific information.
Favorites ▾	Displays a list of your favorite documents so that you can quickly access them. Also includes an Add to Favorites command so that you can add items to your Favorites menu.
Go ▾	Displays a menu that lists the same commands previously described for the Web toolbar.
🔲	Shows only the Web toolbar so that more space is available on your screen to display the document.

Part III

Word 2000

Microsoft Office 2000 comes with the latest and greatest version of the Microsoft premier word processing program, Microsoft Word 2000. (Word 2000 is also known as Word 9.) This part covers the basics of using Word 2000. You can find lots more information about Word 2000 in *Word 2000 For Windows For Dummies,* by Dan Gookin, published by IDG Books Worldwide, Inc.

In this part . . .

- ✔ Formatting your text
- ✔ Creating footnotes and a table of contents
- ✔ Discovering the most useful Word 2000 keyboard shortcuts
- ✔ Using Mail Merge
- ✔ Using themes and styles to simplify formatting chores
- ✔ Working with tabs

Borders

To add a border around a text paragraph, follow these steps:

1. Place the insertion point anywhere in the paragraph to which you want to add a border.

2. Choose Format⇨Borders and Shading to open the Borders and Shading dialog box.

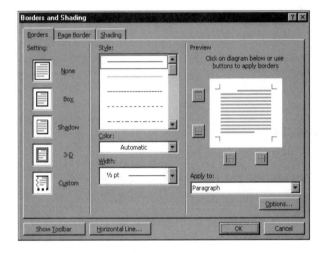

3. Select the type of border you want from the options in the Setting area of the dialog box's Borders tab (Box, Shadow, 3-D, or Custom, for example). Or click None if you want to remove the border.

4. Select a line style from the Style list, a color from the Color list, and a line width from the Width list if you don't like the default settings.

Scroll through the entire list of styles; Word 2000 offers lots of interesting lines from which to choose. If you want each side of the border to have a different style, select the style and then click the appropriate button in the Preview area to apply the style to just that edge. After you change the style, the border around the mock paragraph in the Preview area changes so that you can see how your text appears with the border styles you selected.

5. Click OK or press Enter.

To get rid of a border, choose Format⇨Borders and Shading and then choose None for the border type.

Browsing Through a Document

Word 2000 offers a new Browse control located at the bottom of the scroll bar, as shown in the margin.

After you click the Select Browse Object button sandwiched between the two double-arrow controls, a menu appears that enables you to access several navigation features from one convenient location, as shown in the following figure:

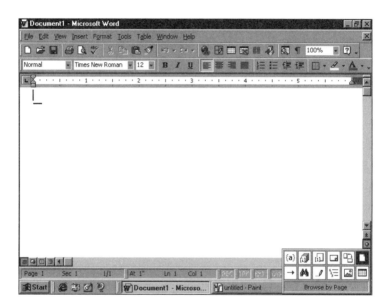

Two of the buttons on this menu invoke the familiar Edit⇨Go to and Edit⇨Find commands. The ten remaining buttons change the unit by which the document is browsed after you click the double up or double down arrow controls immediately above and below the Select Browse Object button. The following table describes the function of each of the 12 buttons that appear on the Browse menu.

Button	What It Does
→	Invokes the Edit⇨Go to command.
🔍	Invokes the Edit⇨Find command.

(continued)

Button	What It Does
	Browse by edits (works in conjunction with revision tracking).
	Browse by headings, as indicated by standard heading styles.
	Browse by graphic objects.
	Browse by Word table objects.
{a}	Browse by Word fields.
	Browse by endnote.
	Browse by footnote.
	Browse by comments.
	Browse by section.
	Browse by page.

Bulleted Lists

To create a bulleted list, follow this procedure:

1. Type one or more paragraphs to which you want to add bullets.

2. Select the paragraphs to which you want to add bullets by dragging the mouse over them.

 3. Click the Bullets button on the Formatting toolbar.

To add additional items to the bulleted list, position the cursor at the end of one of the bulleted paragraphs and press Enter. Because the bullet is part of the paragraph format, the bullet format carries over to the new paragraph.

The Bullets button works like a toggle: Click the button once to add bullets and click the button again to remove them. To remove bullets from an entire list, select all the paragraphs in the list and click the Bullets button.

If you want to create a bulleted list as you compose your text, start by formatting the first paragraph with a bullet. (Either type the text and then format it or create the formatting and then add the text. Word is versatile enough to work both ways.) Word 2000 carries the bullet format over to subsequent paragraphs as you type them. After you finish typing your last bulleted paragraph, press Enter and then click the Bullets button again to "turn off" the bullet format.

To change the appearance of the bullet, choose Format⇨Bullets and Numbering and click the Bulleted tab. If the bullet style you want appears in the Bullets and Numbering dialog box, click that style and then click OK. Otherwise, click the Customize button to summon the Customize Bulleted List dialog box, click Bullet, and then select whichever oddball bullet character makes you happy.

Columns

To create multiple columns in your Word 2000 document:

1. Click the Columns button on the Standard toolbar to open the drop-down menu, as shown in the following figure:

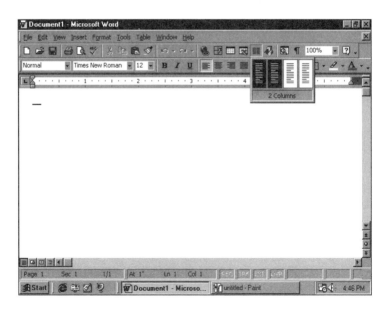

2. Drag the mouse to pick the number of columns you want. For example, if you want three columns in your document, drag the mouse over the columns until three are highlighted.

3. Release the mouse button.

Voilá! The document appears formatted with the number of columns you select.

In normal view (choose View⇨Normal), the text is formatted according to the width of the column, but the columns don't appear on-screen side by side. To see all columns side by side on-screen, switch to Print Layout view by choosing View⇨Print Layout.

For a quick glimpse of how the columns appear after you print them, choose File⇨Print Preview. After you have a good look, click the Close button to return to your document.

The Columns button enables you to set the number of columns, but the button doesn't enable you to control the size of each column or the amount of space between columns. To set the size of the columns and the space between them, choose Format⇨ Columns and play with its settings.

For more information, check out *Word 2000 For Windows For Dummies*.

Document Map

The *Document Map* is a cool feature that enables you to view your document's outline side-by-side with the text, as shown here:

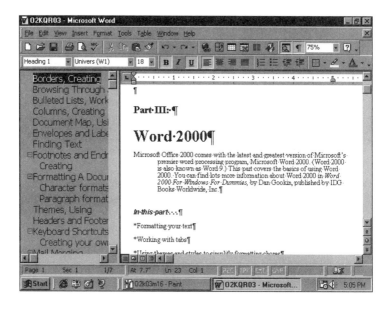

 To show the Document Map, click the Document Map button in the Standard toolbar. The Document Map button works like a toggle: Click it once to summon the Document Map; click it again to send the Document Map into exile.

After the Document Map is open, you can quickly move to any spot in your document simply by clicking the appropriate heading in the Document Map.

Envelopes and Labels

Choosing Tools➪Envelopes and Labels in Word 2000 makes printing addresses on envelopes easy. Here's the blow-by-blow procedure:

1. If you're writing a letter to put in the envelope, create and print the letter first.

Doing so saves you the trouble of typing the mailing address twice.

2. Choose Tools➪Envelopes and Labels.

The Envelopes and Labels dialog box appears.

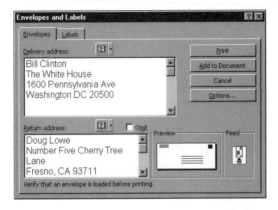

3. Check the address in the Delivery Address field.

Word 2000 can usually automatically find the mailing address from an ordinary letter. If not, you must enter the address yourself.

If you want a return address printed on the envelope, type the return address in the space provided. (Notice that you can set a default return address by using the Tools⇨Options command, clicking the User Info tab, and typing your return address into the space provided there.)

4. Insert an envelope into your printer.

The Feed option in the Envelopes dialog box indicates how you should insert the envelope into the printer. If you want to feed the envelope differently, click the envelope icon in the Feed area of the Envelopes dialog box to open the Envelope Options dialog box. Select the feeding method you prefer and then click OK.

5. Click the Print button.

That's all!

Finding Text

You can choose Edit⇨Find to find text anywhere in a document. Just follow these steps:

1. Choose Edit⇨Find or press Ctrl+F to open the Find and Replace dialog box.

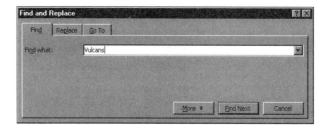

2. In the Fi**n**d What text box, type the text that you want to find.

You can type a single word or a phrase. Spaces are allowed.

3. Click the **F**ind Next button.

4. Wait a second while Word 2000 searches your document.

After Word 2000 finds the text, the program highlights the text on-screen. The Find dialog box remains on-screen so that you can click the Find Next button to find yet another occurrence of the text. After Word 2000 can find no more occurrences of the text, you see the following message in a separate dialog box:

```
Word has finished searching the document.
```

5. Click OK and get on with your life.

You can bail out of the Find and Replace dialog box by clicking the Cancel button or pressing Esc.

You can change how Word 2000 searches for your text by clicking the More button in the Find and Replace dialog box to reveal a set of additional search options. The following options are available:

Search Option	*What It Does*
Search	Enables you to specify the direction in which Word 2000 searches the document for text. The choices are Up, Down, and All. If you choose Up or Down, Word 2000 stops at the beginning or end of the document and asks whether you want to continue the search. If you specify All, Word 2000 automatically searches the entire document.
Match Case	Indicates that whether the text appears in uppercase or lowercase letters matters.
Find Whole Words Only	Finds your text only if the text appears as a whole word. For example, if you type the word **versa**, Word ignores any appearance of *versatile* because the targeted letters are not a whole word.

(continued)

Search Option	What It Does
Find All Word Forms	Searches for all forms of the search text word. For example, if you search for *stink*, Word 2000 also finds *stank* and *stunk*.
Use Wildcards	Enables you to include wildcard characters in the Find What text box. Here are three of the most useful wildcards:
	? Finds a single occurrence of any character. For example, **f?t** finds *fat* or *fit*.
	* Finds any combination of characters. For example, **b*t** finds any combination of characters that begins with *b* and ends with *t*, such as *bat*, *bait*, *ballast*, or *bacteriologist*.
	[abc] Finds any one of the characters enclosed in the brackets. For example, **b[ai]t** finds *bat* or *bit* but not *bet* or *but*.
Sounds Like	Finds text that is phonetically similar to the search text, even if the spelling varies.
Format	Enables you to search for text that has specific formatting applied — for example, to search for text formatted in the Arial font or with red type.
Special	Enables you to search for special characters, such as paragraph or tab marks.

Footnotes and Endnotes

Follow these steps to add footnotes or endnotes to your documents:

1. Place the cursor where you want the footnote reference number to appear in your text.

2. Choose Insert⇨Footnote to open the Footnote and Endnote dialog box.

3. If you want the note to appear at the bottom of the page, check the Footnote option. To create a note that appears at the end of the document, click the Endnote option.

Note: The first time you choose Insert⇨Footnote, the Footnote option is selected. Thereafter, the default setting is whatever you chose the last time you inserted a footnote or endnote. As a result, you need to worry about selecting Footnote or Endnote only if changing from footnotes to endnotes or back again.

4. Click OK.

A separate Footnotes or Endnotes window opens at the bottom of the screen, where you can type your footnote or endnote.

5. Click the Close button that appears in the Footnotes or Endnotes window after you finish typing in the footnote or endnote.

The Footnotes or Endnotes window disappears.

Alternatively, you can just click back in the document to continue editing the document while leaving the Footnotes or Endnotes window open.

Word 2000 automatically numbers footnotes for you and keeps the numbers in sequence as you insert and delete footnotes. Word 2000 also automatically formats footnotes so that a footnote always appears at the bottom of the page in which the footnote is referenced, if possible. Long footnotes span several pages if necessary.

For an extra-quick way to create a footnote, press Ctrl+Alt+F.

To recall the Footnotes window, choose View⇨Footnotes. You can then use the drop-down control that appears in the Footnotes window to display endnotes instead of footnotes.

If you goof up a footnote, double-click the footnote reference in the text. This opens the Footnote window and displays the footnote. You can then edit the note however you see fit.

To delete a footnote, select its footnote reference in the text and press Delete.

For more information about footnotes, see *Word 2000 For Windows For Dummies.*

Formatting a Document

Word 2000 gives you more ways to format your document than any mere mortal would ever need. The following sections present the more common formatting procedures.

Setting the character format

You can set character formats by using the formatting keyboard shortcuts or the buttons which appear in the Formatting toolbar, as described later in this part. Or you can use the following procedure to apply character formats via the Format⇨Font command:

1. Highlight the text to which you want to apply the formatting.

If you skip this step, Word 2000 applies formatting to all new text you type until you repeat the procedure to deactivate the formatting.

2. Choose Format⇨Font.

The Font dialog box appears.

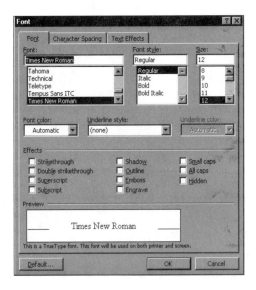

3. Play with the controls in the Font dialog box to set the Font, the Font style (bold, italic, and so on), and the Size; select any of the Effects area check boxes you want (Strikethrough, Superscript, and so on); and use the drop-down list boxes to set the Underline and Font color.

The Preview box at the bottom of the dialog box shows how text appears after Word 2000 applies the formatting options you select.

4. Click OK after you have the character format just the way you want.

You can quickly set character formats by selecting the text to which you want the formats applied and then using one of the buttons on the Formatting toolbar or the keyboard shortcuts listed in the table in the section "Keyboard Shortcuts," later in this part. Alternatively, you can use the keyboard shortcut or click the button to enable the format, type some text, and then use the shortcut or button again to disable the format.

The single fastest way to format a paragraph or character is to use the Format Painter. This works only if you already have some text formatted the way you like. Simply highlight the already formatted text and click on the Format Painter button on the Standard toolbar. Then move your cursor down to the text that you want to look just like the formatted text and highlight it. Word 2000 automatically formats the new text to look just like the previously formatted text. If you have text scattered through your document that you want formatted identically, highlight the text you want to use as your template and then double-click the Format Painter button. The Format Painter continuously formats text that you highlight until you either hit one of the keys, double-click the mouse again, or click the Format Painter button again. If you really like keyboard shortcuts, you can activate the Format Painter by pressing Ctrl+Alt+C, and apply the formatting style to highlighted text by pressing Ctrl+Alt+V.

Setting the paragraph format

Follow these steps to apply paragraph formats by using the Format⇨Paragraph command:

1. Click anywhere in the paragraph you want to format.

You don't need to select the entire paragraph as long as the insertion point is somewhere in the paragraph you want to format.

2. Choose Format⇨Paragraph.

The Paragraph dialog box appears.

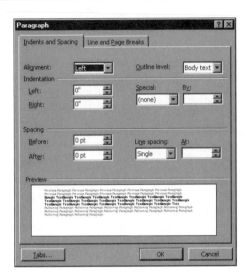

3. Play with the controls to set the paragraph's Alignment, Indentation, and Spacing.

You have lots of controls to play with, and you may not know which to choose. Fortunately, you can monitor the effect of each setting in the Preview box that appears in the Paragraph dialog box.

4. Click OK after you finish formatting your paragraph.

You can quickly set paragraph formats by selecting the paragraphs you want to format and then using one of the buttons on the formatting toolbar or keyboard shortcuts listed in the table in the section "Keyboard Shortcuts," later in this part. To apply the format to a single paragraph, just place the insertion point anywhere in the paragraph.

Headers and Footers

To add a header or footer to a document, follow these steps:

1. Choose View➪Header and Footer.

The Header and Footer toolbar appears, along with the header of the current page. (If you haven't yet created a header for the document, the header area is blank.)

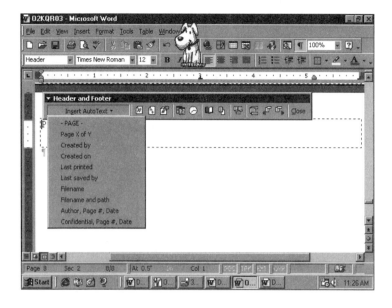

2. To switch between headers and footers, click the Header and Footer button in the toolbar.

3. Type your header or footer text in the header or footer area, formatting the text any way you want.

Insert Auto Text is a new feature for Word 2000. Click this button and to see a drop-down list of the information that is most commonly placed in a header or a footer. You can simply scroll down the list and click the features you want. The information is automatically inserted for you.

4. Click the other buttons in the Header and Footer toolbar to add the page numbers or the date or time. Here's what each button does:

Button	What It Does
	Inserts the number of the current page.
	Inserts the total number of pages in the document.
	Enables you to specify a format for page numbers.
	Inserts the date.

(continued)

Button	What It Does
⊘	Inserts the time.
📖	Opens the Page Setup dialog box with the Layout tab appearing on top. This allows you to control the layout of the headers and footers of the document.
🗐	This hides the document text from your screen while you are working with your headers and footers.
🗐🗐	Sets up the same header or footer as you used previously in the document. This is useful if you need to have different headers or footers in the same document.
🗐	Shows the previous header or footer in the document.
🗐	Shows the next header or footer in the document.
Close	Closes the Header and Footer toolbar.

5. Click the Close button after you finish adding a header or footer.

For more information, see *Word 2000 For Windows For Dummies.*

Keyboard Shortcuts

The following tables list the most useful Word 2000 keyboard shortcuts.

Keyboard shortcuts for editing

Shortcut	What It Does
Ctrl+X	Cuts text to the Clipboard.
Ctrl+C	Copies text to the Clipboard.
Ctrl+V	Pastes text from the Clipboard.
Ctrl+Z	Undoes the most recent command.
Ctrl+Y	Redoes an undone command.
Ctrl+Del	Deletes from the insertion point to the end of the word.
Ctrl+Backspace	Deletes from the insertion point to the start of the word.
Ctrl+F	Finds text.
Ctrl+H	Replaces occurrences of one text string with another text string.
Ctrl+A	Selects the entire document.

Keyboard shortcuts for formatting characters

Shortcut	Button	What It Does
Ctrl+B	**B**	**Bolds** text.
Ctrl+I	*I*	*Italicizes* text.
Ctrl+U	<u>U</u>	<u>Underlines text (continuous).</u>
Ctrl+Shift+W		<u>Underlines words.</u>
Ctrl+Shift+D		<u>Double-underlines text.</u>
Ctrl+Shift+A		Sets the font to ALL CAPS.
Ctrl+Shift+K		Sets the font to SMALL CAPS.
Ctrl+=		Uses subscript font.
Ctrl+Shift+=		Uses superscript font.
Ctrl+Shift+H		Makes the text hidden.
Shift+F3		Changes from uppercase to lowercase and vice versa.
Ctrl+Shift+*		Displays nonprinting characters.
Ctrl+K		Inserts a hyperlink.
Ctrl+Shift+F	Times New Roman	Changes font.
Ctrl+Shift+P		Changes point size.
Ctrl+]		Increases size by one point.
Ctrl+[		Decreases size by one point.
Ctrl+Shift+>		Increases size to next available size.
Ctrl+Shift+<		Decreases size to preceding available size.
Ctrl+Shift+Q		Switches to Symbol font (Greek Tragedy).
Ctrl+Shift+Z		Removes character formatting.
Ctrl+spacebar		Removes character formatting.

Keyboard shortcuts for formatting paragraphs

Shortcut	Button	What It Does
Ctrl+L		Left-aligns a paragraph.
Ctrl+R		Right-aligns a paragraph.
Ctrl+J		Justifies a paragraph.
Ctrl+E		Centers a paragraph.
Ctrl+M		Increases left indent.
Ctrl+Shift+M		Reduces left indent.
Ctrl+T		Creates a hanging indent.
Ctrl+Shift+T		Reduces a hanging indent.
Ctrl+1		Single-spaces a paragraph.
Ctrl+2		Double-spaces a paragraph.
Ctrl+5		Sets line spacing to 1.5.
Ctrl+0 (zero)		Removes or sets space before a line to one line.
Ctrl+Shift+S	Normal	Applies a style.
Ctrl+Shift+N		Applies Normal style.
Ctrl+Alt+1		Applies Heading 1 style.
Ctrl+Alt+2		Applies Heading 2 style.
Ctrl+Alt+3		Applies Heading 3 style.
Ctrl+Shift+L		Applies List style.
Ctrl+Q		Removes paragraph formatting.
		Formats a numbered list.
		Formats a bullet list.

Assigning your own keyboard shortcuts

In the event that Word 2000 doesn't supply enough keyboard shortcuts to fill your needs, you can easily create your own shortcuts. You can assign your own keyboard shortcuts to styles, macros, fonts, AutoText entries, commands, and symbols. Just follow these steps:

1. Choose Tools⇨Customize to open the Customize dialog box.

2. Click on the Commands tab and click on the Keyboard button on the bottom of the dialog box.

The Customize Keyboard dialog box now appears, as shown in the following figure:

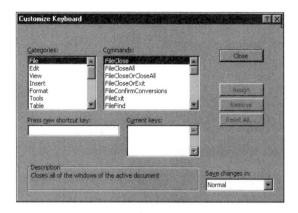

3. Select the command, style, macro, font, or other item for which you want to create a keyboard shortcut by using the Categories and Commands lists.

4. Click the Press new shortcut key box and then type the new keyboard shortcut.

5. Click the Assign button to assign the keyboard shortcut and then click the Close button.

You can also assign keyboard shortcuts by clicking the Shortcut Key button from the dialog box that appears after you choose Insert⇨Symbol or click the Modify button in the Style dialog box, which appears after you choose Format⇨Style⇨Modify.

To reset all keyboard shortcuts to their Word 2000 defaults, choose Tools⇨Customize, click the Keyboard button in the Customize dialog box to summon the Customize Keyboard dialog box, and then click the Reset All button.

Mail Merging

Mail Merge is one of the most tedious of all Word 2000 tasks. Fortunately, the Mail Merge Helper stands by, ready to help you at a moment's notice. Mail Merge is a three-step process: First, you create the form letter (in Word 2000 Speak, the *main document*);

then you create a mailing list of names and addresses *(the data source)*; and finally, you merge the form letter and the mailing list to create a letter for each person on your mailing list. The following sections spell out the procedures for each step in detail.

Creating the main document

Here's the procedure for creating a main document to use in a mail merge:

1. Choose Tools⇨Mail Merge.

The Mail Merge Helper dialog box appears.

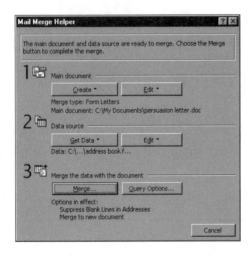

2. Click the Create button and then choose Form Letters from the drop-down list that appears.

The following dialog box appears.

3. Click the New Main Document button to open the Mail Merge Helper dialog box.

4. Click the <u>E</u>dit button to reveal a menu of documents you can edit.

The menu should have only one entry, Form Letter: Document #.

5. Click this selection to create the letter.

6. Type the letter any way you want, but leave blanks where you want Word 2000 to insert personalized data later, such as in the inside address or the salutation (**Dear ,**).

When you edit a mail merge main document, a special Mail Merge toolbar appears above the Standard toolbar. Some of the buttons on this toolbar you use in later steps.

7. Choose <u>F</u>ile⇨<u>S</u>ave to save the file after you're done.

Your letter should look something like the one shown here:

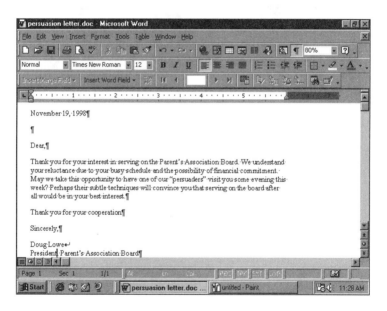

Creating the data source

The next big step in Mail Merge is creating the data source, which may be the hardest part of the procedure, because creating a data source requires you to type in all the names and addresses of those to whom you want the form letter sent. This bothersome procedure is as described in the following steps:

1. Choose Tools⇨Mail Merge.

The Mail Merge Helper dialog box returns to life.

2. Click the Get Data button and then choose Create Data Source from the menu that appears.

The Create Data Source dialog box appears.

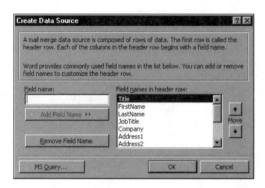

3. To add a field, type a name in the Field name text box and then click the Add Field Name button.

4. To remove a field, click the field in the Field names in header row list to select the field and then click the Remove Field Name button.

5. To change the order in which the fields appear, select the field you want to move in the Field names in header row list and then click the up-arrow or down-arrow Move button to move the field.

6. Click OK after you're satisfied with the fields listed for inclusion in the data source.

The Save As dialog box appears.

7. Type an appropriate name for your mailing list document in the File name text box and then click the Save button.

A dialog box appears to inform you that the data source is empty.

8. Click the Edit Data Source button in the dialog box that appeared in Step 7 to begin adding names and addresses to the data source.

A Data Form dialog box appears, similar to the one shown in the following figure:

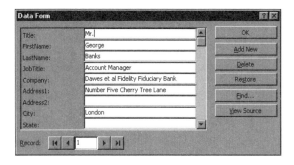

9. Type the information for one person you want to add to the data source.

Use the Tab key to move from field to field or to skip over those fields in which you don't want to enter any data. (You don't need to enter a value for every field.)

10. After you type all the data for the person, click the Add New button to add that person's data to the table in the data source.

11. Repeat Steps 9 and 10 for each person that you want to add to the data source.

12. After you add all the names that you want to add, click OK.

Notice that you can use the arrow buttons at the bottom of the Data Form dialog box to move forward or backward through the data source records. Thus you can recall a previously entered record to correct a mistake if necessary.

To delete a record, use the arrow buttons at the bottom of the Data Form dialog box to move to the record you want to delete and then click the Delete button.

Inserting field names in the main document

After you finish adding names and addresses to the data source, return to the main document. (Because the main document is still open, you can select it from the Window menu.) Now you need to add field names to the main document so that Word 2000 knows where to insert data from the data source into the form letter. Here's the procedure:

1. Position the insertion point where you want to insert a field from the data source.

2. Click the Insert Merge Field button on the Mail Merge toolbar.

A menu of field names from the data source appears.

3. Click the name of the field that you want to insert into the document.

4. Repeat Steps 1 through 3 for each field that you want to insert.

The following figure shows what a document looks like with all the fields inserted:

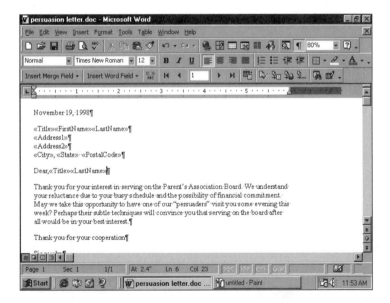

5. After you finish inserting fields, choose File⇨Save to save the file.

Merging the documents

After you set up the main document and the data source, you're ready for the show. Follow these simple steps to merge the main document with the data source to produce form letters:

1. Choose Tools⇨Mail Merge to open the Mail Merge Helper dialog box.

2. Click the Merge button.

The Merge dialog box appears.

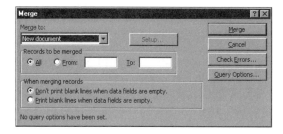

3. Click the Merge button.

Word 2000 creates a new document that contains one complete copy of the main document for each record in the data source, with data from the data source substituted for each merge field. The merged copies are separated from one another by section breaks.

4. Scroll through the merged document to make sure that the merge worked the way you expected.

5. To save the merged document, choose File⇨Save.

Saving the file is a good idea, but be warned that the file may be quite large, depending on how many records you merged from the data source.

6. To print the merged document, choose File⇨Print.

Numbered Lists

To create a numbered list, follow this procedure:

1. Type one or more paragraphs that you want to number.

2. Select all the paragraphs that you want to number.

3. Click the Numbering button on the Formatting toolbar.

If you add or delete a paragraph in the middle of the numbered list, Word 2000 renumbers the paragraphs to preserve the order. If you add a paragraph to the end of the list, Word 2000 assigns the next number in sequence to the new paragraph.

The Numbering button works like a toggle: Click the button once to add numbers to paragraphs; click the button again to remove them. To remove numbering from a numbered paragraph, place the insertion point anywhere in the paragraph and click the Numbering button. To remove numbering from an entire list, select all the paragraphs in the list and click the Numbering button.

If you insert a nonnumbered paragraph in the middle of a numbered list, Word 2000 breaks the list in two and begins numbering from one again for the second list. If you simply turn off numbering for one of the paragraphs in a list, however, Word 2000 suspends the numbering for that paragraph and picks up where the sequence left off for the next numbered paragraph.

For more advanced numbering options, choose Format➪Bullets and Numbering and then choose the Numbered or Outline Numbered tabs.

Replacing Text

You can choose Edit➪Replace to replace all occurrences of one bit of text with other text. Here's the procedure:

1. Press Ctrl+Home to get to the top of the document.

If you skip this step, the search-and-replace operation starts at the position of the insertion point.

2. Choose Edit➪Replace or press Ctrl+H to open the Find and Replace dialog box with the Replace tab active.

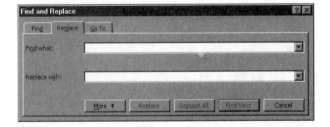

3. Type the text you want to find in the Find What box and then type the text you want to substitute for the Find What text in the Replace With box.

4. Click the Find Next button.

After Word 2000 finds the text, the program highlights the text on-screen.

5. Click the Replace button to replace the text.

6. Repeat Steps 4 and 5 until you finish searching the document. Word 2000 displays a message to tell you that it is finished.

As for the Find command, you can click the More button to display additional options such as Match Case, Find Whole Words Only, Use Wildcards, Sounds Like, and Find All Word Forms options. See the section "Finding Text," earlier in this part, for details.

If you're absolutely positive that you want to replace all occurrences of your Find What/Replace With text, click the Replace All button. This feature automatically replaces all occurrences of the text. The only problem is that you're bound to encounter at least one spot where you don't want the replacement to occur. Replacing the word *mit* with *glove*, for example, changes *Smith* to *Sgloveh.* (And no, Sgloveh is *not* the Czechoslovakian form of the name Smith.)

If you do click the Replace All button, Word 2000 displays an informative message at the end of the replacement procedure, indicating how many replacements were made. If this number seems unreasonable to you (for example, you thought the document contained only three occurrences of the Find what text, but Word 2000 says that it made 257 changes), choose Edit⇨Undo to undo all the replacements in one fell swoop.

Selecting Text

You can select text in a document in many ways by using the mouse or the keyboard.

Selecting text by using the mouse

Here are the common mouse actions for selecting text:

✦ Drag the mouse over the text you want to select.

✦ Click the mouse at the start of a block of text, press and hold the Shift key, and then click again at the end of the block. This procedure selects everything in between the clicks.

✦ Double-click to select a single word.

✦ Triple-click to select an entire paragraph.

✦ Press and hold the Ctrl key and then click to select an entire sentence.

✦ Press and hold the Alt key and then drag the mouse to select any rectangular area of text.

✦ Click the selection bar (the invisible vertical area to the left of the text) to select a line.

✦ Double-click the selection bar to select an entire paragraph.

Selecting text by using the keyboard

You can use the following keyboard techniques to select text:

✦ Place the cursor at the beginning of the text you want to select, press and hold the Shift key, and then move the cursor to the end of the text you want to select by using the cursor-control arrow keys. Release the Shift key after you select the text you're interested in.

✦ Press Ctrl+A to select the entire document.

✦ Press F8 and then press any key to extend the selection to the next occurrence of that key's character. For example, to select text from the current location to the end of a sentence, press F8 and then press the period key.

You can keep extending the selection by pressing other keys. For example, if you press the period key again, the selection is extended to the next period. To stop extending the selection, press the Escape key.

Styles

Styles are one of the best ways to improve your word processing efficiency. A style is a collection of paragraph and character formats that you can apply to text in one fell swoop. The most common examples of styles are for headings. By using a style to format your headings, you can make sure that all headings are formatted in the same way. And you can quickly change the appearance of all headings by simply changing the style.

Applying a style

To apply a style to a paragraph, follow these steps:

1. Put the cursor in the paragraph you want to format.

2. Select the style you want from the style box on the Formatting toolbar.

(The style box is the first drop-down list box control on the Formatting toolbar.)

To apply a style to two or more adjacent paragraphs, just select a range of text that includes all the paragraphs you want to format. Then select the style.

If the style you want doesn't appear in the style list, press and hold the Shift key and then click the down arrow next to the style box. Word 2000 lists only the most commonly used styles if you don't hold down the Shift key.

For more information on styles, see *Word 2000 For Windows For Dummies.*

Creating a style

To create a new style, follow these steps:

1. Tweak a paragraph until the text is formatted just the way you want.

Set the font and size, line spacing, before and after spacing, and indentation. Also set tabs and any other formatting you want, such as bullets or numbers. You can set these formatting options by using either the controls on the Formatting toolbar or the commands on the Format menu.

2. Click anywhere in the paragraph on which you want to base the style and then press Ctrl+Shift+S or click the style box on the Formatting toolbar.

3. Type a descriptive name for the style.

4. Press Enter to add the style to the list of styles for the document.

Alternatively, you can choose Format⇨Style to summon the Style dialog box and then click the New button. A New Style dialog box that enables you to set all the formatting options for a new style appears.

For more information, see *Word 2000 For Windows For Dummies.*

Table of Contents

To create a table of contents, make sure that you format your document's headings by using the Word 2000 heading styles (Heading 1, Heading 2, and Heading 3). If you use the heading styles, creating a table of contents is easy. Here's the procedure:

1. Move the insertion point to the place in your document where you want the table of contents to appear.

2. Choose Insert⇨Index and Tables.

The Index and Tables dialog box appears.

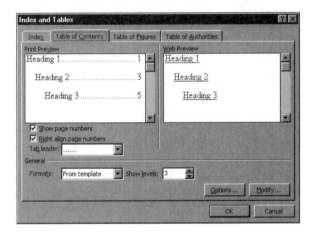

3. Click the Table of Contents tab.

4. Pick the Table of Contents style you want from the Formats list.

5. Play with the other controls to fine-tune the table of contents.

The following table describes the other controls of this dialog box.

Option	What It Does
Show page numbers	Clear this check box if you want the TOC to show the document's outline but not page numbers.
Right align page numbers	Clear this check box if you want the page numbers to be placed right next to the corresponding text rather than at the right margin.
Show levels	Use this control to set the amount of detail included in the table.
Tab leader	Select the tab leader style you want to use.

6. Click OK.

Word 2000 inserts the TOC into your document at the insertion point.

If the table of contents looks like {TOC \o "1-3" \p " "}, choose Tools⇨Options to open the Options dialog box, click the View tab, and click the Field codes check box to remove the check mark. Click OK, and the table appears as it should.

If you edit a document after creating a table of contents, you can update the table of contents to make sure that its page numbers are still correct. Select the table by clicking it anywhere with the mouse and then press F9.

Tables

Tables are a nifty feature of Word 2000 that enable you to organize information into a grid similar to that of a spreadsheet. Two ways are available to create tables in Word 2000: The old fashioned way, by using the Table⇨Insert Table command, or the new way, which uses a fancy command called Draw Table.

Tables a la the Insert Table command

Word 2000 includes a friendly Insert Table command that enables you to create tables by using any of several predefined formats. Here is the procedure:

1. Position the insertion point where you want to insert the table into your document.

2. Choose Table⇨Insert Table.

An Insert Table dialog box appears.

3. Select the size of the table by setting the Number of columns and Number of rows text boxes.

4. Click the AutoFormat button to open the Table AutoFormat dialog box.

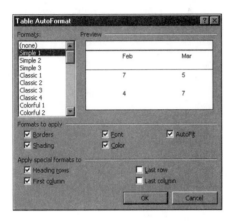

5. Choose the format you want to use for the table from the list of Formats.

6. Specify any other options you want to apply to the table, such as which formats to apply or whether to use special formatting for the first row or column.

7. Click OK to close the Table AutoFormat dialog box and then click OK to create the table.

There is a faster way to Insert a table into your document. Simply click the Insert Table button. This produces a drop-down box that shows a grid of columns and rows. Drag your cursor diagonally across the drop-down box to highlight the number of rows and columns you want in your table. When you release the mouse button, your table is inserted at the current cursor position.

After you create a table, you can type data into its cells by clicking the cell where you want to enter data and typing the data. You can use the arrow keys to move from cell to cell in any direction you want, or you can press the Tab key to move to the next cell in the table.

Tables via the Draw Table command

The Draw Table command is a feature that enables you to draw complicated tables on-screen by using a simple set of drawing tools. The Draw Table command is ideal for creating tables that aren't merely a simple grid of rows and columns but rather boast a complex conglomeration of cells, in which some cells span more than one row and others span more than one column. These types of tables were difficult to create in Word 95, but Word 2000 enables you to create such tables with just a few mouse clicks. Here's the procedure:

1. Choose Table⇨Draw Table or click the Tables and Borders button on the Standard toolbar. You can also get to this toolbar by clicking View⇨Toolbars⇨Tables and Borders.

Word 2000 switches into Page Layout View (if you aren't already there) and opens the Tables and Borders toolbar.

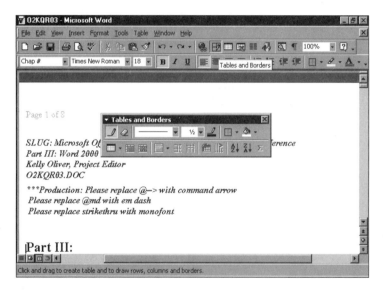

2. Draw the overall shape of the table by dragging the mouse to create a rectangular boundary for the table. Point the mouse where you want one of the corners of the table to be and then press and hold the mouse button while dragging the rectangle to the opposite corner.

After you release the mouse button, a table with a single cell appears, as shown in the following figure:

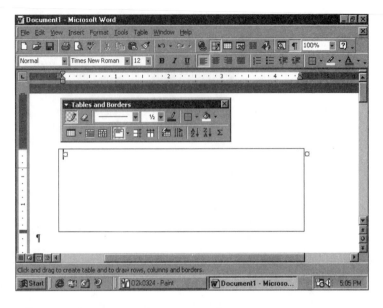

3. Carve the table up into smaller cells.

> To split the table into two rows, for example, point the mouse somewhere along the left edge of the table, press and hold the mouse button, and then drag a line across the table to the right edge. After you release the mouse, the table splits into two rows, as shown in the following figure:

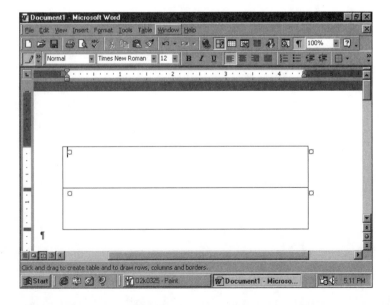

You can continue to carve up the table into smaller and smaller cells. For each slice, point the mouse at one edge of where you want the new cell to begin and drag the mouse to the other edge. If you want to change the line size or style drawn for a particular segment, you can use the line style and size drop-down controls in the Tables and Borders toolbar. You can change the style of a line you've already drawn by tracing over the line with a new style. The following figure shows some of the possibilities available in creating your table:

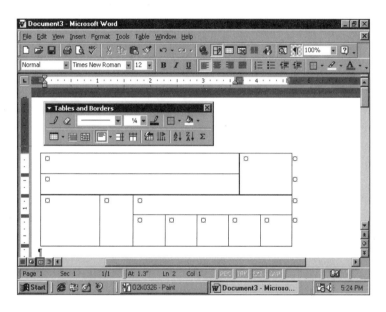

4. After you finish creating your table, click the Tables and Borders button again to close the Tables and Borders toolbar.

You can then type data into any of the table's cells by clicking the cell to select it and typing the data.

Tabs

The following sections list the most common procedures for working with tabs.

Setting tabs

Here's the procedure for setting tabs by using the ruler, which sits atop the document window. (If the ruler isn't visible, use the View⇨ Ruler command to reveal it.) Follow these steps:

1. Type some text that you want to line up with tab stops.

2. Select the paragraph or paragraphs for which you want to set tabs.

3. Click the ruler at each spot where you want a new tab stop.

4. Adjust the settings the way you want.

5. Return to your text and add the tabs at the appropriate places.

To adjust a tab setting, just use the mouse to grab the tab marker in the ruler and slide the tab to the new location. (If you can't find the ruler, choose View⇨Ruler.) After you release the mouse button, text in the currently selected paragraphs adjusts to the new tab position.

Default tab stops lie every 0.5 inch in the ruler. Each time you create a new tab stop, however, Word 2000 deletes all default tab stops to the left of the new tab stop. In other words, default tab stops continue to exist only to the right of new tab stops you create.

Word 2000 enables you to create four types of tab alignments: *left*, *center*, *right*, and *decimal*. To change the type of tab that you created as you click the ruler, click the Tab Alignment button at the far-left edge of the ruler. Each time you click this button, the picture on the button changes to indicate the alignment type, as follows:

✦ **Left tab:** Text left-aligns at the tab stop.

✦ **Center tab:** Text centers over the tab stop.

✦ **Right tab:** Text right-aligns at the tab stop.

✦ **Decimal tab:** Numbers align at the decimal point over the tab stop.

To remove a tab stop from the ruler, click the tab stop you want to remove and drag the tab off the ruler. After you release the mouse button, the tab stop disappears.

To remove all tab stops quickly, choose Format⇨Tabs and then click the Clear All button in the Tabs dialog box.

For more information, see *Word 2000 For Windows For Dummies.*

Creating leader tabs

Leader tabs have rows of dots instead of spaces between tab stops. (Leader tabs are common in tables of contents and indexes.) Here's the procedure for creating leader tabs:

1. Set a tab stop by using the procedure described in the section "Setting tabs."

2. Choose Format⇨Tabs.

The Tabs dialog box appears.

3. Choose the leader style by selecting option 2, 3, or 4 in the Leader area.

4. Click OK.

Now, after you press the Tab key, a row of dots or a solid line appears.

For more information, see *Word 2000 For Windows For Dummies.*

Templates

Suppose that you toiled for hours on a document, and now you want to make its styles, macros, and other goodies available to other documents you may someday create. You can do that by creating a *template.* Then, if you create a new document based on your template, that document inherits the styles, AutoText entries (portions of prerecorded text that you can call up with just a few mouse clicks), macros, and text from the template. Here's how to create a template:

1. Open the document that has all the styles, AutoText, macros, and other goodies you want to save in a template.

2. Choose File⇨Save As to open the Save As dialog box.

3. In the Save as type list box (way down at the bottom of the Save As dialog box), select Document Template as the file type.

4. In the File Name text box, type a filename for the template.

Don't type the extension; Word 2000 takes care of that element.

5. Click the Save button to save the document as a template file.

6. Delete any unnecessary text from the file.

Any text that you do not delete appears automatically in any new documents you create based on the template.

7. Save the file again.

You can also create a template by choosing File⇨New and then clicking the Template radio button in the New dialog box. Doing so creates an empty template based on the template you select in the dialog box. You can then modify the template as you see fit and save that template under a new name.

For more information, see *Word 2000 For Windows For Dummies.*

Themes

Themes are a new feature in Word 2000. A theme is sort of like a template; it defines the fonts and style of your documents. However, there are significant differences. Themes do not automatically include macros, AutoText, or customized settings. What themes do give you that is different from a template is a unified design scheme that can include background images, fonts, bullets, horizontal lines, and other design elements. Using themes allows you to create consistently professional-looking documents, and they are especially good for Web page design.

If you don't like any of the themes that come with Word 2000 and don't want to go through the work of creating your own, there are more available online. Simply click Help⇨Microsoft on the Web and follow the directions to download more themes onto your computer.

Applying a theme to a document

To start your document with a theme already applied, follow these steps:

1. With the document open, select Format⇨Theme.

The Theme dialog box opens. It doesn't matter whether you've already worked on the document or are just starting. Just make sure that there is an active cursor within the document screen and that no text is highlighted.

2. The Theme dialog box shows you a list of available themes in the Choose a Theme window on the left, and the window on the right will display a sample of the themes. Scroll through the list and look at the samples until you find one you like.

3. In the lower-left corner are three checkboxes that allow you to refine your control of the theme. These three boxes are Vivid Colors, Active Graphics, and Background Image. Play with turning these three boxes on and off to see how they affect the look of your document, and until you find the look you want.

4. Click OK.

If you've just begun working with your document, it applies the styles appropriate for the theme you've chosen as you write. If you're applying the theme to a document you've worked on, it changes your formatting to match the theme.

You can mix and match themes with predetermined styles. At the bottom of the Theme dialog box is the Style Gallery button. If you click this button, the Style Gallery dialog box opens. From this dialog box, you can choose different styles and see what your document will look like using that style with the theme you've chosen. Nifty, eh?

Changing the default theme

Word 2000 has a default theme that it applies to all documents when they are first open. You can change this default so that a new theme always appears whenever you open a new Word document. To do this:

1. Click Format⊅Theme to open the Theme dialog box as usual.

2. Determine what theme you want in the same manner as described in Applying a Theme, and click the Set Default button.

A dialog box appears asking you if you want to set a new default theme for new documents.

3. If you really want to do this, click Yes.

4. Click OK in the Theme dialog box.

From now on, every new Word 2000 document you create will have that theme applied to it, until you decide to change it.

Web Page Wizard

Do you want to make yourself known on the World Wide Web with your own Web page, but are afraid that you're not enough of a geek for the complex HTML programming? Fear not! Word 2000 comes with a slick Web Page Wizard that can automatically create several different types of Web documents based on options you select. Trust me; anyone who can create a Word document can create a Web site using the Web Page Wizard. To use the Wizard, follow these steps:

1. Choose File⊅New.

2. After the New dialog box appears, click the Web Pages tab, click Web Page Wizard, and then click OK.

The Web Page Wizard dialog box appears.

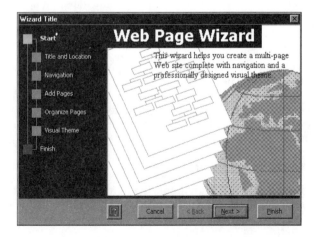

3. Click the Title and Location button on the left side of the window or click Next to move to the next screen on the list.

This allows you to give your site a title (which also functions as its file name) and the location where you want to save it on your system.

4. When you have entered that information, click the Next button.

5. Click the Navigation button.

A dialog box that allows you to determine how your readers can navigate through the links in your Web page opens. You have three options, which are:

- **Vertical frame.** This divides your screen with a vertical line. On the left are the links, which, when clicked, show the content on the right side of the screen.

- **Horizontal frame.** Divides the screen into a top half and a bottom half. The links appear on the top, while the content is displayed in the bottom half.

- **Separate page.** Probably the form of navigation that I'm most familiar with. Every time a link is activated, it opens a new page to display the information.

Choose the option that works best for you; however, be aware that not all browsers can support vertical or horizontal frames, so the Separate page option is probably your best bet.

5. After you've made your choice, click the Next button.

The next screen shows the Add Pages portion of the Web Page Wizard. With this feature, you can select what types of documents are associated with your Web page.

You can use Add New Blank Page for plain text, Add Template Page for specific Web templates (such as FAQ, Tables of Contents, or columns), and Add Existing File, which allows you to add any document from your computer system.

6. Select those pages you want to include and then click Next.

The Organize Pages feature allows you to determine the order in which the individual pages appear on your Web site. Simply highlight one of the pages and then click on either the Move Up or the Move Down button to position it where you want. Repeat with the different pages until everything is in the order you want.

7. Click <u>N</u>ext.

This screen allows you to apply a visual theme to your document or keep it simple with a plain white background. Themes are discussed in "Themes," earlier in this part.

8. After you've determined what theme you are using, click <u>N</u>ext again.

That's it! Your Web page is organized and ready for you to enter the information you want on it.

9. Click the <u>F</u>inish button, and the document appears on your screen.

To find out more information about designing Web pages, **_see also_** Part IX, "Completing Complex Tasks," in this book.

For even more complete knowledge of Web sites and how to build them, please look at *Word 2000 For Windows For Dummies*.

Part IV

Excel 2000

Excel 2000 is the bean counter of Microsoft Office 2000. It enables you to create spreadsheets that can perform meticulous calculations with uncanny accuracy. This part covers the basics of using Excel 2000. If you're interested in going beyond the basics, you can find more information in *Excel 2000 For Windows For Dummies,* by Greg Harvey, published by IDG Books Worldwide, Inc.

In this part . . .

- ✔ **Creating great-looking charts**
- ✔ **Formatting cells**
- ✔ **The most useful Excel 2000 functions**
- ✔ **Working with pivot tables**
- ✔ **Using styles with your spreadsheet**

AutoFormatting

You can efficiently create an attractively formatted worksheet by using the AutoFormat feature to apply predefined formatting to your worksheet. Here's how:

1. Create your worksheet as you normally would.

The AutoFormat feature works best when the first row and the first column of the worksheet contain headings and the last row contains totals because many of the AutoFormats apply special formatting to the first row and column. The last column of the worksheet may also contain totals, but it doesn't have to. The AutoFormats work whether the last column contains totals or not. They also work if the first row and column do not contain headings, but you may have to remove the special formatting for the first row and column.

2. Highlight the entire range of worksheet cells that contains data you want to format, as shown in the following figure:

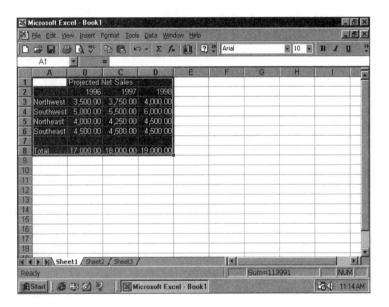

3. Choose Format⇨AutoFormat.

The AutoFormat dialog box appears, as shown in the following figure:

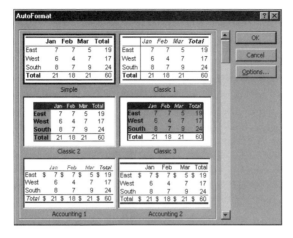

4. Select the table format you want to use from the choices shown in the dialog box.

5. Click OK.

Excel 2000 applies the selected AutoFormat to your worksheet, as shown in the following figure:

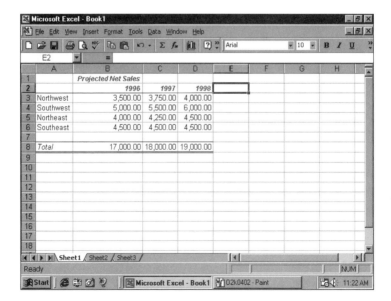

If you don't like the formatting applied by the AutoFormat, press Ctrl+Z, choose Edit ⇨Undo, or click the Undo button to undo the AutoFormat operation.

Centering Text over Several Columns

You may frequently want to center text over several columns. Suppose, for example, that you put projected net sales for 1996, 1997, and 1998 in columns B, C, and D, respectively, and actual net sales for 1996, 1997, and 1998 in columns E, F, and G. Wouldn't having a Projected Net Sales heading centered over the projected net sales columns and an Actual Net Sales heading centered over the actual net sales columns be a really nice touch?

You can accomplish this effect by merging cells from the three columns to create a single cell that spans several columns. Here is the procedure:

1. Move the cell pointer to the leftmost cell in the range of columns over which you want to center the text.

For example, if you want text centered over the range B2:D2, move the cell pointer to cell B2. (See the section "Referencing Spreadsheet Cells," later in this part, if the notation B2:D2 confuses you.)

2. Enter the text that you want to center into the cell you have selected.

3. Highlight the range of cells across which you want the text centered.

 4. Click the Merge and Center button.

The result should look like the example shown in the following figure. (In this example, both the Projected Net Sales and the Actual Net Sales headings are centered.)

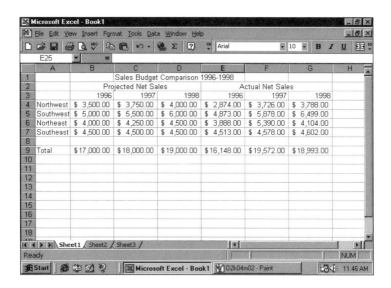

If you change your mind and don't want to center the text across columns, highlight the merged cell, choose Format⇨Cells to bring up the Format Cells dialog box, and deselect the Merge Cells check box on the Alignment tab.

Charting

Excel 2000 offers so many charting capabilities that I could write an entire *Quick Reference* just on charting. Here's the short procedure for quickly creating a simple chart:

1. Select the cells that contain the data on which you want to base a chart.

 2. Click the ChartWizard button on the Standard toolbar.

The Chart Wizard comes to life, as shown in the following figure:

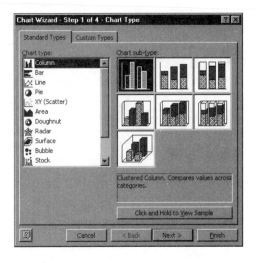

3. From the Chart Type list, select the type of chart you want to create.

For each chart type, you can choose from several sub-types. To see a preview of how the selected data appears charted with a particular chart type, select that chart type from the list and click and hold the mouse button on the Click and Hold to View Sample button.

4. Click the Next button.

5. Check the range shown in the Data range box to verify that the range listed is the range you want to chart.

The Chart Wizard initially assumes that the data you are trying to chart is grouped by row. In other words, the first row of the range contains the first series of values, the second row contains the second series, and so on. If this isn't the case, you can click the Columns radio button so that the data is grouped by column, with the first data series in the first column of the range, the second series in the second column, and so on.

6. Click the Next button.

The following version of this dialog box appears:

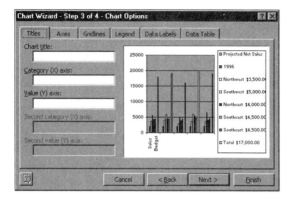

7. Add any optional features to your chart by filling in the text boxes and setting various option buttons that appear on the Chart Options version of the Chart Wizard dialog box.

Notice that the Chart Options dialog box has six tabs that display various charting options. Be sure to check the settings on all six tabs before proceeding.

For example, you can include a title for the chart by typing a title into the Chart Title text box.

The changes you make to the settings on the Chart Options dialog box appear in the preview area, which takes up the entire right side of the dialog box. This preview gives you an idea of how each setting affects the chart's appearance.

8. Click the Next button.

The Chart Wizard displays its final dialog box.

9. Choose where you want Excel 2000 to place your chart — as a new sheet or as an object in any sheet in the current workbook — and then click the Finish button to create the chart.

If you add the chart to an existing sheet, you may need to drag and possibly resize the chart to its correct location and size.

A new feature in Excel 2000 is that after you add a chart to your spreadsheet as an object, you can summon a toolbar to your screen that allows you to continue to manipulate the chart. There are buttons to change the grouping of the data, to angle your text, to add, format, or remove the legend, or even to change the chart type. This toolbar allows you to play with the chart to your heart's content without having to return to the Wizard to make a new chart. To open this toolbar, select View➪Toolbars➪Chart.

Comments

Excel 2000 enables you to add an electronic version of those yellow sticky notes to your worksheets. You can use this feature as a reminder to yourself and others who may use the worksheet, such as a reminder about why you created a formula the way you did or where you got a particular number you entered into the worksheet. Just follow these steps:

1. Click the cell to which you want to add the note.

2. Choose Insert➪Comment or press Shift+F2.

A yellow, balloon-style box appears.

3. Type anything you want in the box.

You can, for example, question the value listed in the cell, as shown in the following figure:

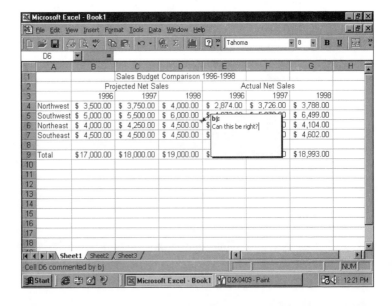

4. Click anywhere outside the yellow comment balloon.

The comment balloon disappears, and Excel 2000 adds a colored marker to the cell to indicate that a comment is attached to that cell.

To access the comment later, simply point to the cell; the comment balloon appears. The balloon disappears after you move the mouse pointer away from the cell.

To delete a comment, right-click the cell and choose Delete Comment from the pop-up menu that appears.

Conditional Formatting

Conditional formatting allows you to format a cell or a range of cells to have specific formatting dependent upon the value or formula in that cell. To do this:

1. Highlight the cell or range of cells that you want to have formatted.

2. Click Format➪Conditional Formatting.

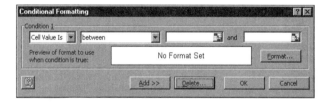

3. In the drop-down box on the left, select whether you want the formatting to be used when a cell value is determined or if a particular formula is active within a cell.

The appearance of the dialog box changes to match this condition.

4. If you want to use a formula, type the formula in the text box provided.

Remember that every formula must begin with an =.

If you are using a cell value, you have to determine how the condition relates to the statement. The second drop-down box on the left allows you to determine if the condition to be met is between, equal to, greater than, less than, or any one of several other relationship statements. Select the one that you want. For example, if you want to see all cells that have a value of more than $19,000.00, select "greater than" from this drop-down box. Type in the value you want to compare the number in the cell against in the text box provided.

5. After you have the cell value or formula set, click the Format button.

The Format Cells dialog box opens.

6. Apply the formatting you want and click OK.

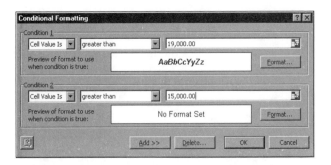

Conditional formatting allows you to set multiple conditions for formatting on a cell or range of cells. You can have one set of formatting if the numbers in the cell indicate that you met minimum expectations, but you can show an entirely different formatting if the numbers indicate that you met or exceeded your goals.

7. Click the Add button.

A dialog box showing Condition 2 appears.

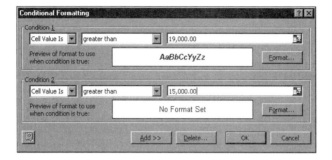

There is one thing you need to be aware of when you are setting more than one condition for a cell. This feature is activated whenever the program determines that the condition you've established is "True." If more than one condition is True, then only the first one will be applied. All the others will be ignored. The way to deal with this is to set the most difficult condition first. If, for example, you want the numbers in the Totals row to be italicized if they meet your sales quota ($15,000 in the previous figure) but to be in bold italics if they meet your personal sales goal ($19,000), then set the more less-likely number (the personal sales goal) first.

8. After you've established the conditions and formatting for that particular cell, or range of cells, click OK and move on.

Finding Lost Data

You can choose Edit⇨Find to find text anywhere in a worksheet. Just follow these steps:

1. Press Ctrl+Home to move to the top of the worksheet.

This step is optional; if you omit it, the search starts at the current cell.

2. Use the Edit⇨Find command or press Ctrl+F to summon the Find dialog box.

3. Type the text you want to find in the Find What text box.

4. Click the Find Next button.

When Excel 2000 finds the cell that contains the text you're looking for, it highlights the cell. The Find dialog box remains on-screen so that you can click Find Next to find yet another occurrence of the text.

After Excel 2000 finds the last occurrence of the text, it resumes its search again from the top. This process goes on forever, until you bail out by clicking Close or pressing Esc.

The Find dialog box offers several options for controlling the search, as described in the following table.

Option	What It Does
Search	Indicates whether you want to search by rows or columns.
Look In	Indicates whether you want to search cell values, formulas, or notes attached to cells.
Match Case	Finds only text with the case (uppercase and lowercase letters) that matches the search text you type.
Find Entire Cells Only	Finds text only if the entire cell entry matches the Find What text.

You can use the following wildcard characters in the Find what text box:

✦ ? finds a single occurrence of any character. For example, **f?t** finds *fat* and *fit*.

✦ * finds any combination of characters. For example, **b*t** finds any combination of characters that begins with *b* and ends with *t*, such as *bat, bait, ballast,* and *bacteriologist.*

If you find the text you're looking for and decide that you want to replace it with something else, click Replace. This action opens the Replace dialog box.

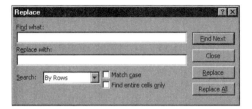

You can then type replacement text in the Replace With text box, and then click Replace to replace a single occurrence of the Find text or Replace All to replace the Find text wherever it appears in the document.

Formatting a Cell or Range of Cells

You can set formats for a cell or range of cells by using formatting keyboard shortcuts or by using the formatting controls on the Formatting toolbar. Or you can use the following procedure to apply character formats by using the Format➪Cells command:

1. Highlight the cell or cells to which you want to apply the formatting.

2. Choose Format➪Cells or use the handy keyboard shortcut, Ctrl+1.

Either way, the Format Cells dialog box appears, as shown in the following figure:

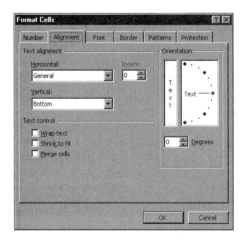

3. Play with the controls under the six tabs to set the formatting options that you want.

4. Click the OK button after you format the cells the way you want.

Functions

The following table details some common Excel 2000 functions. The program has hundreds of other functions that you can use, but these are the most common. For information on how to insert a function, see the section "Function Wizard," later in this part.

Command	Explanation
ABS(*number*)	Returns the absolute value of *number. Number* is usually a cell reference, as in ABS(B3), or the result of a calculation, such as ABS(D19-D17).
AVERAGE(*range*)	Calculates the average value of the cells in *range* by determining the sum of all the cells and then dividing the result by the number of cells in the range. Excel 2000 doesn't count blank cells, but the program does count cells that contain the value zero.
COUNT(*range*)	Returns the number of cells in *range.* Excel 2000 doesn't count blank cells, but the program does count cells that contain the value zero.
HLOOKUP(*lookup_value, table_array, row_index_num*)	Searches for the cell in *table_array* that contains the value specified by *lookup_value.* HLOOKUP searches all the cells in the first row of the range specified for *table_array.* If the function finds *lookup_value*, HLOOKUP returns the value of the corresponding cell in the row indicated by *row_index_num.* To return the value in the corresponding cell in the second row of the table, for example, specify **2** for *row_index_num.*
IF(*logical_test, value_if_true, value_if_false*)	Tests the condition specified in the logical test. If the condition is true, Excel 2000 returns *value_if_true.* Otherwise, the program returns *value_if_false.*
LOWER(*text*)	Converts the *text* to lowercase.
MAXIMUM(*range*)	Returns the largest value in *range.*

Command	Explanation
MEDIAN(*range*)	Returns the median value of the cells in *range*. If you sort the cells in order, the median value is the value in the cell that falls right in the middle of the sorted list. Half the cell values are larger than the median value, and the other half are smaller.
MINIMUM(*range*)	Returns the smallest value in *range*.
NOW()	Returns the current date and time. No arguments are required.
PMT(*rate, nper, pv*)	Calculates payments for a loan. *Rate* is the interest rate per period; *nper* is the number of periods; *pv* is the present value (that is, the amount of the loan). Make sure that you specify the interest rate for each period and the total number of periods. If, for example, the annual interest rate is 12 percent and you make payments monthly, the periodic interest rate is 1 percent. Likewise, if the loan is for three years and you make payments monthly, 36 periods exist.
PRODUCT(*range*)	Multiplies all the cells in the specified *range*.
PROPER(*text*)	Converts the text to proper case, in which the program capitalizes the first letter of each word in *text*.
ROUND(*number, decimal places*)	Rounds off the number to the specified number of decimal places. For example, ROUND(C1,2) rounds off the value in cell C1 to two decimal places.
SUM(*range*)	Adds the values of all cells in the specified *range*.
SUMPRODUCT (*range1, range2*)	Multiplies each cell in *range1* by its corresponding cell in *range2* and then adds the resulting products together.
TODAY()	Returns the current date. No arguments are required.
UPPER(*text*)	Converts the *text* to uppercase.
VLOOKUP(*lookup_value, table_array, col_index_num*)	Searches for the cell in *table_array* that contains the value specified by *lookup_value*. VLOOKUP searches all the cells in the first column of the range specified for *table_array*. If the function finds *lookup_value*, VLOOKUP returns the value of the corresponding cell in the column indicated by *col_index_num*. To return the value in the corresponding cell in the second column of the table, for example, specify **2** for *col_index_num*.

Function Wizard

The easiest way to insert a function is to use the Function Wizard. The Function Wizard asks you to select a function from one of several function categories and to complete the function by providing all the information the function requires.

Here's the procedure, using a simple MAX function as an example:

1. Move the cell pointer to the cell in which you want to insert the function.

2. Choose Insert⟹Function.

The Paste Function dialog box appears. The Paste Function dialog box initially lists the functions you used most recently.

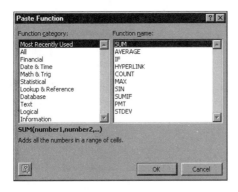

3. If the function that you want to insert in the cell appears in the Function Name list, click to select the name of the function; otherwise, click one of the categories in the Function Category list and then select the function from the Function Name list.

4. Click OK.

A dialog box appears, similar to the one in the following figure:

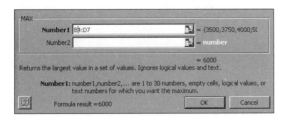

5. Read the instructions for completing the function and then
type whatever entries you need to complete the function.

If the function requires just a single argument, Excel 2000 uses
the cell or range that was selected at the time you accessed
the Function Wizard. This means that you don't need to do
anything in this dialog box except click OK.

 If the function requires more than one argument, you can type a
value, cell reference, or range into the text boxes for the
additional arguments. If you want, you can mark a cell or range
of cells in the spreadsheet by clicking the button that appears
to the right of the text box for the argument you want to enter.
This action returns you to the spreadsheet, where you can mark
the cell or range. Press Enter to return to the Function Wizard;
the range you marked appears in the text box for the argument.

6. Click OK after you complete the function.

For more information about specific functions, see the section
"Functions," earlier in this part.

Moving Around Your Worksheet

You can move around a worksheet easily enough by using the
mouse; just click the cell you want to move to. See Part II for more
information on moving around with the mouse.

The following table summarizes the keyboard techniques you can
use for moving around a worksheet.

Shortcut	What It Does
Home	Moves to the beginning of the current row.
PgUp	Scrolls the window up one screen.
PgDn	Scrolls the window down one screen.
Alt+PgDn	Scrolls the window right one screen.
Alt+PgUp	Scrolls the window left one screen.
Ctrl+End	Moves to the last cell of the worksheet that contains data.
Ctrl+Home	Moves to the beginning of the worksheet.
Ctrl← or End,←	Moves to the left of a data block.
Ctrl+→ or End,→	Moves to the right of a data block.
Ctrl+↑ or End,↑	Moves to the top of a data block.
Ctrl+↓ or End,↓	Moves to the bottom of a data block.
Ctrl+PgUp	Switches to the preceding sheet in the same workbook.

(continued)

Shortcut	What It Does
Ctrl+PgDn	Switches to the next sheet in the same workbook.
End, Home	Moves to the last cell in the worksheet that contains data.
End, Enter	Moves to the last cell in the current row that contains data.
Ctrl+G	Goes to a specific location.

Naming a Range of Cells

To make your formulas easier to understand, Excel 2000 enables you to assign meaningful names to individual cells or cell ranges. Here's the procedure for assigning a name to a cell or range of cells:

1. Select the cell or range of cells to which you want to assign a name.

2. Choose Insert⇨Name⇨Define to open the Define Name dialog box, as shown in the following figure:

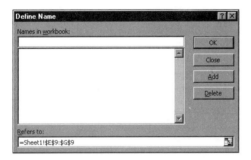

3. Type a name for the cell or cell range in the Names in Workbook text box.

You have some restrictions on what you can use for a name for your cells. To be acceptable, the name cannot have any spaces in it, must use only alphanumeric characters (no symbols), and must start with at least one letter, even if the rest of the "name" is numeric.

4. Click OK to close the Define Name dialog box.

To use a range name in a formula, type the name anytime you would type a range. Instead of typing **=Sum(F4:F15)**, for example, you can type the formula **=Sum(SalesTotals)**.

To delete a range name, choose Insert⇨Name⇨Define to open the Define Name dialog box, select the range name that you want to delete from the list, and then click the Delete button.

You can quickly select a named range by either pressing F5 or choosing Edit⇨Go To to open the Go To dialog box and then double-clicking the range name in the list box.

Pivot Tables

A *pivot table* is a slick way of summarizing information that is stored in an Excel 2000 worksheet or an Access database. You can use pivot tables with worksheets in which information is stored in rows, where each column represents a field.

Suppose, for example, that you are charged with tracking fund-raising activities of a group of students. Each row in a worksheet can represent a single fund-raising activity for a particular student, with columns for the student's name, the fund-raising activity, the amount raised, and the month in which the activity occurred. Such a worksheet may look like the example in the following figure:

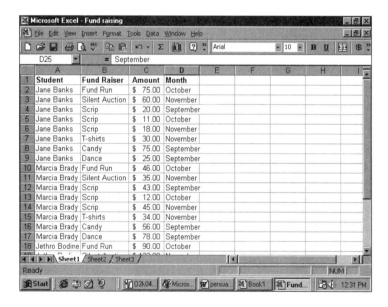

To create a pivot table from a worksheet such as this, follow these steps:

1. Select a cell within the worksheet's table that you want to serve as the basis for the pivot table.

Which cell you select doesn't matter, as long as the cell is within the table on the worksheet.

2. Choose Data⇨PivotTable and PivotChart Report to open the PivotTable and PivotChart Wizard, as shown in the following figure:

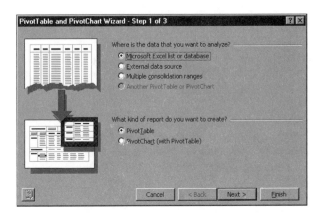

3. Leave the data source option set to Microsoft Excel List or Database and click the Next button to proceed.

Step 2 of the PivotTable and PivotChart Wizard appears, as shown in the following figure. If you selected a cell within the table before starting the PivotTable and PivotChart Wizard, Excel 2000 should correctly guess the range of cells on which to base the pivot table. If not, you can change it here.

4. If the correct range appears in the Range text box, click Next to move on to Step 3 of the PivotTable and PivotChart Wizard.

5. Determine whether you want the pivot table to be constructed in the same worksheet or in a new worksheet.

(If you choose a new worksheet, it will still exist in the same file, and you can switch between the sheets by clicking the tabs on the bottom-left corner of your screen.)

6. Click the Layout button.

The Layout dialog box of this Wizard opens, as shown in the following figure:

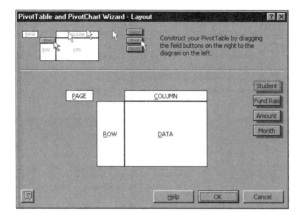

Each column in the table appears as a field button in the PivotTable and PivotChart Wizard.

7. Pick the field that contains the data you want to summarize and drag the button for that field into the Data area of the pivot table.

In the Fund Raising table, for example, you drag the Amount field to the Data area.

8. Drag the other fields to the Row, Column, or Page areas, depending on how you want to summarize the data.

For the Fund Raising example, I dragged the Student button to the Column area, the Fund Raiser button to the Row area, and the Month button to the Page area.

After Excel 2000 creates the pivot table, you can move these fields around to change how Excel 2000 summarizes the data. Here's how the PivotTable Wizard may appear after the fields have been dragged into the pivot table:

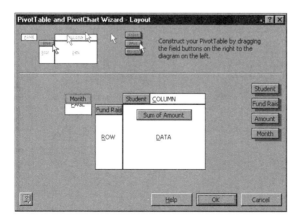

9. Click OK to return to Step 3.

10. Click Finish to close the PivotTable and PivotChart Wizard and to look at the pivot table.

Here's how the pivot table should look after Excel 2000 finishes its work:

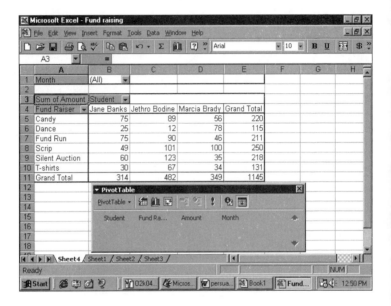

You can change how Excel 2000 summarizes the pivot table's information by dragging the field buttons to different locations in the table. If, for example, you'd rather see each student's fund-raising activities summarized by month, drag the fields around so that the table appears as shown in the following figure:

Printing a Worksheet

Printing in Excel 2000 is pretty much the same as printing in any other Office 2000 application: You can choose File➪Print, press Ctrl+P, or click the Print button in the Standard toolbar to print the current worksheet. Excel 2000, however, offers a few printing tricks that you should know about:

✦ By default, Excel 2000 prints the entire worksheet. However, you can set a print area to print just part of the worksheet. First, highlight the range you want to print. Then choose File➪Print Area➪Set Print Area.

✦ To clear the print area so that the entire worksheet prints, choose File➪Print Area➪Clear Print Area.

✦ If annoying grid lines appear on your printed output, choose File➪Page Setup to summon the Page Setup dialog box. Click the Sheet tab and then click Gridlines to remove the check mark. Click OK to dismiss the Page Setup dialog box.

Referencing Spreadsheet Cells

Like other spreadsheet programs, Excel 2000 uses a standard notation to refer to cells within a worksheet. Each column in a worksheet is assigned a letter — A, B, C, and so on. Columns beyond column Z use two letters, so the columns that come next after column Z are columns AA, AB, AC, and so on. Rows are numbered, starting with 1.

Each cell is given an *address* that is a combination of its column letter and row number. Thus the cell at the intersection of column E and row 5 is cell E5.

A *range* of cells is a rectangular area that is identified by two cells at opposite corners, separated by a colon. Thus the range C7:E10 is all the cells in a rectangle with its upper-left corner at cell C7 and lower-right corner at E10.

You sometimes see cell addresses that use dollar signs ($), such as D$9, $E7, or H22. The dollar sign designates the row or column portion of an address as *absolute,* meaning that Excel 2000 shouldn't try to adjust the address if you move or copy a formula that includes the absolute address. For example, suppose that you type the formula =**D3+D4** into cell D5 and then copy cell D5 to cell E5; Excel 2000 adjusts the formula to =E3+E4. But if you make the formula in cell D5 =**$D3+$D4**, Excel 2000 does *not* adjust the formula if you copy it to another column.

One trick you can use with Excel 2000 is that the program can use labels that appear above a column of numbers as cell addresses. For example, suppose you set up a spreadsheet as shown in the following example:

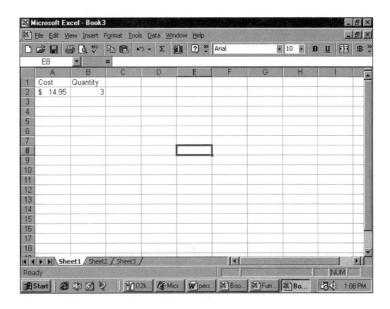

To create a formula in cell C2 that multiplies cells A2 and B2, you could enter **=A2*B2**. With Excel 2000, however, you can enter the formula as **=Cost*Quantity**. Excel uses the column headings in row 1 to figure out that *Cost* is cell A2 and *Quantity* is cell B2.

Styles

Excel 2000 gives you the option of applying styles to your worksheet (or to portions of your worksheet) to create a unified and professional looking design. Unlike AutoFormat, the Styles feature allows you to select from a limited choice of previously designed styles, or you can design your own.

Applying a style

To apply a style to your worksheet:

1. Highlight the cell or cells that you want to format with a particular style.

2. Select Format⇨Style.

The Style dialog box opens, as shown here:

3. Click the Style Name drop-down list to see your selections. Choose one that works for you.

4. Click OK, and your designated cells are formatted with the appropriate style.

Creating a style

To create a new style for your worksheets:

1. Highlight the cell or range of cells that you want to format with the new style.

2. Select Format⇨Style.

3. In the Style Name drop-down list, type a name for your style.

4. In the Style Includes section of the dialog box, click those features that you want included in the new style.

5. Click the Modify button. The Format Cells dialog box opens.

6. Move through the six tabs of this dialog box, and determine what features you want in your new style.

7. Click OK to return to the Style dialog box. The dialog box now shows the features of your new style, as shown in the following figure:

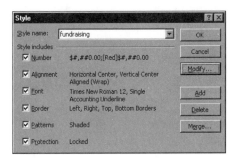

8. Click OK and look at the new style on your spreadsheet.

Unfortunately, you can only use this style within the spreadsheet where you created it. If you want it in a different spreadsheet, you can either re-create it from scratch, or you can use the Format Painter to copy the style in its original document and copy it to the new spreadsheet.

Part V

PowerPoint 2000

If you like to stand in front of a group of people with a flip chart and a pointer, either trying to get them to buy something from you or convincing them to vote for you, then you'll love PowerPoint 2000. PowerPoint 2000 creates presentations that can be printed out on plain paper, made into transparencies or slides, or shown on-screen as an online presentation.

This part shows how to perform the most common PowerPoint 2000 chores. For more complete information about using PowerPoint 2000, get a copy of my book, *PowerPoint 2000 For Windows For Dummies,* published by IDG Books Worldwide, Inc.

In this part . . .

- ✓ Using transitions and effects to create animated slides
- ✓ Adding clip art
- ✓ Working with color
- ✓ Using the AutoContent Wizard to create new presentations
- ✓ Using keyboard shorcuts
- ✓ Creating notes
- ✓ Displaying presentations
- ✓ Publishing your presentation on the Web
- ✓ Finding lost slides
- ✓ Creating summary slides
- ✓ Using the PowerPoint 2000 Viewer

Animating a Slide

Animation allows you to add movement to your slides, which can help keep your audience awake. Every object on a slide can have its own animation effect. You can control the order in which objects are animated and whether animations are manually controlled or happen automatically after a certain time has passed. To add animation to your presentation, follow these steps:

1. Make sure you are in Normal View and scroll to the slide you want to animate.

2. Choose Slide Show⇨Custom Animation. The Custom Animation dialog box appears.

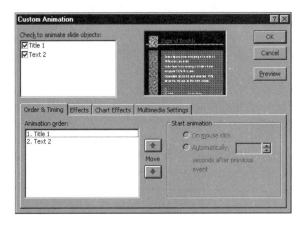

3. Set your options on the Order & Timing tab. Click the slide element you want to animate (such as Title or Text).

If you want the animation to occur automatically, click Automatically in the Start animation part of the dialog box (located in the lower-right corner) and then set the number of seconds you want to pass before the animation starts. If you want the animation to occur when the user clicks the mouse, click On Mouse Click.

4. Click the Effects tab to choose which animation effects you want.

5. When you finish selecting your animation settings for an object, you can see the effect by clicking Preview. PowerPoint demonstrates the effect in the window of the dialog box. Remember, you can only preview the animation effect of one object at a time.

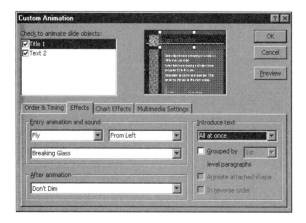

- In the Entry animation and sound group, you can choose how an object appears, such as Fly from Left, Crawl from Right, Dissolve, or Wipe Down. You can also specify a sound to be played when the object enters the slide.

- In the After animation box, you can tell PowerPoint 2000 what to do with the object after the animation: Hide the object, dim the object, change the object to a specified color, hide the object after you click the mouse, or do nothing.

- In the Introduce text grouping, you can set three methods for text to appear: all at once, by words, or by letters. If you want the animation for text objects to be applied in reverse order, allowing you to build slides from the bottom up, check the In reverse order check box. For text objects, you can have the animation apply separately to each paragraph, or you can group paragraphs based on their outline level by checking the Grouped by level paragraphs box and choosing a level in the drop-down list.

6. Repeat Steps 3 and 4 for any other objects you want to animate.

7. After you make all your selections, click OK.

You can also add slide transition effects that are applied as each slide is displayed. For more information, see the section "Transitions," later in this part.

There are three other ways to apply basic animations to slide objects:

✦ The most popular animation settings can be applied by choosing Sli<u>d</u>e Show⇨<u>P</u>reset Animations.

✦ In Slide Sorter view, a drop-down list shows the most popular animation settings. Just right-click the slide you want to animate and choose Preset Animation from the drop-down list. A second list appears that provides you with a list of preset options. Choose the setting you want from the drop-down list.

✦ Choose <u>V</u>iew⇨<u>T</u>oolbars⇨Animation Effects to summon the Animation Effects toolbar, which contains buttons that apply several common animation effects with a single mouse click.

Clip Art

Here is the procedure for adding clip art from the Office 2000 clip art collection to your presentation:

1. Move to the slide that you want to decorate with clip art.

If you want the clip art to appear on every slide, move to the master slide by choosing <u>V</u>iew⇨<u>M</u>aster⇨<u>S</u>lide Master.

 2. Choose <u>I</u>nsert⇨<u>P</u>icture⇨<u>C</u>lip Art or click the Insert Clip Art button found on the Drawing toolbar.

The Clip Gallery dialog box pops up.

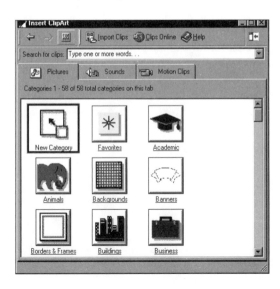

3. Select the category from the Clip Art list box that contains the picture you want.

4. Select the specific picture you want.

Clip Gallery shows several pictures at a time, but you can see other pictures from the same category by scrolling through the pictures. When the picture you want comes into view, click it.

5. When you click one of the Clip Art objects, a drop-down list of buttons appears. Click the Insert clip button.

PowerPoint 2000 sticks the picture right in the middle of the slide, which is probably not where you want it. You can move it and resize it by dragging it with the mouse.

The first time you use Clip Gallery after installing PowerPoint 2000, Clip Gallery realizes that it hasn't added the PowerPoint 2000 clip art to the gallery, so it automatically adds the clip art. This process may take a while, so be prepared.

 Notice that Clip Gallery has tabs for sounds and videos as well as clip art. You can use these tabs to add sounds and movies to your presentations, following the same procedure to select the clip you want to insert.

 If your computer has an Internet connection, you can click the Connect to Web button to connect to Microsoft's clip art page on the World Wide Web to obtain additional clip art pictures, sounds, and videos.

 For more information, see Chapter 11 of *PowerPoint 2000 For Windows For Dummies.*

Color Schemes

A presentation's *color scheme* is a set of coordinated colors that are used for various elements of the presentation's slides, such as the slide background, title text, body text, and so on. You can easily change a presentation's color scheme by following this procedure:

1. If you want to change the color scheme for an entire presentation, switch to Slide Master view by choosing <u>V</u>iew⇨<u>M</u>aster⇨ <u>S</u>lide Master. To change the color scheme only for a specific slide, switch to Normal view by choosing <u>V</u>iew⇨<u>N</u>ormal and go to the slide you want to change.

2. Choose Format⇨Slide <u>C</u>olor Scheme to summon the Color Scheme dialog box.

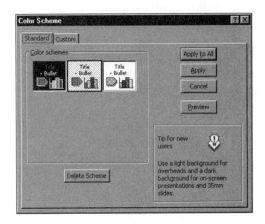

3. Click the color scheme you want to use.

4. Click the Apply <u>t</u>o All button.

To customize the color scheme, click the Custom tab and then choose whatever colors you would like to use for various slide elements.

Creating a New Presentation

The easiest way to create a new PowerPoint 2000 presentation is to use the AutoContent Wizard. Here is the procedure:

1. Start PowerPoint 2000 by clicking the Start button in the taskbar (usually found at the bottom left of the screen).

If it isn't at the top of your Start menu, choose <u>P</u>rograms⇨Microsoft PowerPoint. PowerPoint 2000 comes to life and displays the following dialog box:

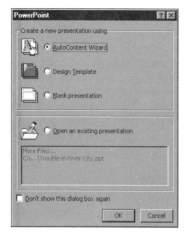

If you already have PowerPoint running, you can get to the AutoContent Wizard by clicking File ⇨New and selecting the AutoContent Wizard from the General tab.

2. Click the AutoContent Wizard radio button and then click OK.

The AutoContent Wizard comes to life.

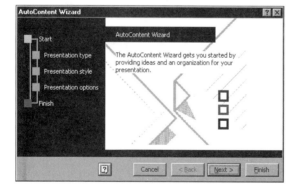

3. Click the Next button.

AutoContent Wizard asks what type of presentation you want to create. To see a full list of the options, click the All button.

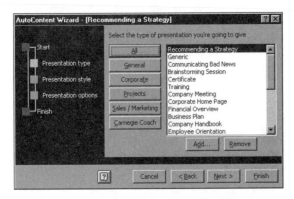

4. Select the presentation you want to create from the list box and then click the Next button.

The Wizard asks what kind of output you want to create for the presentation. This depends on how the presentation will be used. You have several choices, depending on whether it is a live presentation (on-screen presentation, black and white overheads, color overheads, or 35mm slides) or an online presentation (called a Web presentation).

5. Select the type of presentation you're using and then click the Next button.

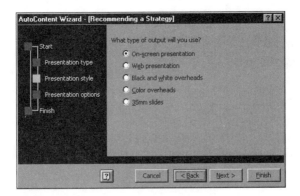

6. Select the output options you want and then click the Next button.

The Wizard demands to know the presentation title and what elements to include on each slide, including a footer, the date you updated your presentation, and whether you want your slides numbered.

7. Type the requested information in the appropriate fields and then click the Next button.

The Wizard displays its final screen.

8. Click the Finish button to create the presentation.

Hiding Background Objects

A *slide master* is a model slide layout that governs the appearance of all the slides in a presentation. PowerPoint 2000 lets you add background objects to the slide master so that the objects appear on every slide in your presentation. For example, you can create a fancy logo or some other slick graphic effect to add spice to your slides.

Occasionally, though, you may want to create a slide or two that doesn't have these background objects. To do so, you must hide the background objects by following this procedure:

1. In Normal view, display the slide you want to show with a plain background.

2. Choose Format➪Background.

The Background dialog box appears.

3. Check the Omit background graphics from master check box.

4. Click the Apply button or press Enter.

This procedure for hiding background objects applies only to the current slide or notes page. Other slides or notes pages are not affected.

You can hide background objects for all slides by calling up the Format➪Background command, checking the Omit background graphics from master check box, and then clicking the Apply to All button.

Keyboard Shortcuts

The following tables list the most useful keyboard shortcuts in PowerPoint 2000. These are shortcuts that are specific to PowerPoint, many of the shortcuts that can be used in all Office programs are explained in "Shortcuts that Work Everywhere" in Part II.

Keyboard shortcuts for editing slides

Shortcut	What It Does
Ctrl+Delete	Deletes from the insertion point to the end of the word.
Ctrl+Backspace	Deletes from the insertion point to the beginning of the word.
Ctrl+M	Inserts a new slide by using the AutoLayout dialog box.
Ctrl+Shift+M	Inserts a new slide without using the AutoLayout dialog box.
Alt+Shift+D	Inserts the date on the Slide Master.
Alt+Shift+T	Inserts the time on the Slide Master.
Alt+Shift+P	Inserts the page number on the Slide Master.
Ctrl+D	Duplicates the selected objects.
Ctrl+←	Moves the insertion point one word to the left.
Ctrl+→	Moves the insertion point one word to the right.
Ctrl+↑	Moves the insertion point to the preceding paragraph, except in Outline view, in which it moves to the preceding slide.
Ctrl+↓	Moves the insertion point to the next paragraph, except in Outline view, in which it moves to the next slide.
Ctrl+End	Moves the insertion point to the end of the page.
Ctrl+Home	Moves the insertion point to the top of the page.
Ctrl+Alt+PgUp	Moves to the preceding slide in Slide Sorter view.
Ctrl+Alt+PgDn	Moves to the next slide in Slide Sorter view.

Keyboard shortcuts for formatting text

Shortcut	What It Does
Ctrl+Shift+F	Activates the font control in the Formatting toolbar so you can change the font.
Ctrl+Shift+P	Activates the font size control on the Formatting toolbar so you can change the point size.
Ctrl+Shift+>	Increases the point size to the next available size.

Shortcut	What It Does
Ctrl+Shift+<	Decreases the point size to the preceding size.
Ctrl+L	Left-aligns the paragraph.
Ctrl+R	Right-aligns the paragraph.
Ctrl+J	Justifies the paragraph.
Ctrl+E	Centers the paragraph.

Keyboard shortcuts for working with outlines

Shortcut	What It Does
Alt+Shift+←	Demotes the selected paragraphs.
Alt+Shift+→	Promotes the selected paragraphs.
Alt+Shift+↑	Moves the selected paragraphs up.
Alt+Shift+↓	Moves the selected paragraphs down.
Alt+Shift+A	Shows all text and headings.
Alt+Shift+−	Collapses all text under a heading.
Alt+Shift++	Expands all text under a heading.
/ (on numeric keypad)	Hides or shows character formatting.

Notes

PowerPoint 2000 enables you to create separate notes to accompany your slides to help you remember what you want to say. The beauty of notes is that the audience doesn't see them, so they think you are winging it when in fact, you are relying on your notes. You can print notes pages that include a small image of the complete slide along with the notes for that slide. To add notes to a slide, follow this procedure:

1. In Normal view, find the slide you want to add notes for.

2. Click in the Click to Add Notes window near the bottom of your screen.

3. Add the text you want in this window.

4. To see your Notes page, select View⇨Notes Page.

5. Adjust the zoom factor with the Zoom drop-down list on the Standard toolbar, if necessary, so you can read the notes text.

6. If necessary, scroll the display to bring the notes text into view.

(The notes text appears beneath the slide image.)

7. If you want to add more text, click in the notes area and type to your heart's content.

The text you type appears in the notes area. You can use any of the PowerPoint 2000 standard word processing features, such as cut, copy, and paste, as you create your notes. Press Enter to create new paragraphs.

After you switch to Notes Page view, you don't have to return to Normal view to add notes for other slides. Use the scroll bar or the PgUp and PgDn keys to add notes for other slides.

For more information, see Chapter 18 of *PowerPoint 2000 For Windows For Dummies.*

Presentations

Here's the procedure for displaying a slide show:

1. Click the Slide Show View button.

The first slide in your presentation appears.

2. To advance to the next slide, press Enter, press the spacebar, or click the left mouse button.

3. Press Esc to end the slide show.

During the slide show, you can use the following keyboard tricks:

To Do This	Press Any of These Keys
Display next slide	Enter, spacebar, right arrow, down arrow, PgDn, N
Display previous slide	Backspace, left arrow, up arrow, PgUp, P
Display first slide	1+Enter
Display specific slide	Slide number+Enter
Toggle screen black	B, period
Toggle screen white	W, comma
Show or hide pointer	A, = (equals)
Erase screen doodles	E
Stop or restart automatic show	S, + (plus)
Display next slide even if hidden	H
Display specific hidden slide	Slide number of hidden slide+Enter
Change pen to arrow	Ctrl+A
Change arrow to pen	Ctrl+P
End slide show	Esc, Ctrl+Break, – (minus)

To set up a presentation so that it runs continuously on the computer, choose Slide Show➪Set up show to summon the Set Up Show dialog box. Check the Loop Continuously until 'Esc' option and the Using Timings, if Present option, and then click OK. Then click Slide Show➪Rehearse Timings. This opens the slide show with a timer dialog box that lets you manually set the timing for your slide show. As soon as it opens, the timer starts counting. Determine how long you want the slide to remain on the screen; when you reach that time, click on the Next arrow. The screen will move to the next slide on the sequence and start all over again. When you get to the end of the slides, a dialog box appears asking whether you want to use these timings. If you're happy with the timings, click Yes. The screen opens to Slide Sorter view, which allows you to see the times you've set for each slide.

Rearranging Slides

You can quickly rearrange slides by switching to Slide Sorter view, in which you can see a thumbnail version of each slide in a presentation. Here's the procedure:

 1. Switch to Slide Sorter view by clicking the Slide Sorter View button at the bottom-left corner of the screen or by choosing View➪Slide Sorter.

PowerPoint 2000 switches to Slide Sorter view, as the following figure shows:

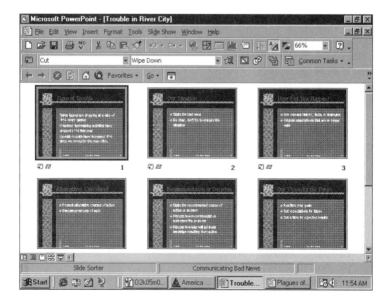

2. To move a slide, click and drag it to a new location.

   PowerPoint 2000 adjusts the display to show the new arrangement of slides and automatically renumbers the slides.

3. To delete a slide, click the slide and press the Delete key or choose Edit⇨Delete Slide.

   (The Delete key works on an entire slide only in Slide Sorter view.)

4. To add a new slide, click the slide that you want the new slide to follow and then click the Insert New Slide button to summon the New Slide dialog box (or you can select Insert⇨New Slide). Then click the slide layout you want to use and click OK to insert the slide. To edit the contents of the slide, return to the Normal view.

If your presentation contains more slides than fit on-screen at the same time, you can use the scroll bars to scroll the display. Or you can change the zoom factor to make the slides smaller. Click the down arrow next to the zoom size, and select a smaller zoom percentage.

Recurring Text

To add recurring text to each slide, follow this procedure:

1. Call up the Slide Master by selecting View⇨Master⇨ Slide Master.

2. Click the Text Box button on the Drawing toolbar.

3. Click where you want to add text.

4. Type the text that you want to appear on each slide.

5. Format the text however you want.

6. Return to Normal view.

To add a graphic that recurs on each slide, click the Insert Clip Art button on the Standard toolbar to insert any clip art picture supplied with PowerPoint 2000 or choose Insert⇨Picture to insert a picture file.

To delete an object from the Slide Master, click it and press Delete. To delete a text object, you must first click the object and then click the object frame again. Then press Delete.

If the object won't select when you click it, you probably fell back into Normal view. Click View⇨Master⇨Slide Master again to call up the Slide Master.

Slide Finder

Slide Finder is a feature that helps you quickly copy slides from other presentations into your presentation. Slide Finder can search presentations that are stored on your hard disk or on presentations that are stored on other computers on a network. To use Slide Finder, follow these steps:

1. In Normal or Slide Sorter view, move to the location where you would like to insert a slide stolen from another presentation.

2. Choose <u>I</u>nsert⇨Slides from <u>F</u>iles.

The Slide Finder dialog box appears.

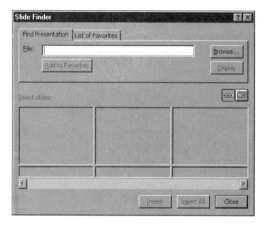

3. Click the <u>B</u>rowse button to summon the Insert Slides from Files dialog box shown in the following figure:

4. Locate the file you want to copy slides from and click the Open button to return to the Slide Finder dialog box.

5. Click the Display button.

The Slide Finder dialog box displays the slides in the presentation.

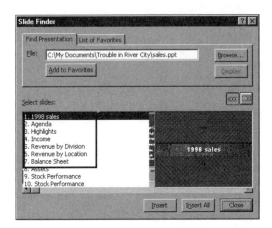

6. Select the slide you want to insert.

Use the scroll bar if necessary.

7. Click the Insert button.

8. Repeat Steps 6 and 7 if you want to copy additional slides from the presentation.

9. Click the Close button after you insert all the slides you need.

Summary Slides

You can quickly create a summary slide that contains the titles of some or all of the slides in your presentation by following these steps:

1. Switch to Slide Sorter view.

2. Select the slides you want to include in the summary.

To summarize the entire presentation, press Ctrl+A to select all the presentation's slides.

 3. Click the Summary Slide button.

It's on the Slide Sorter toolbar, which appears at the top of the screen, beneath the Formatting toolbar. PowerPoint 2000 inserts the summary slide in front of the selected slides.

Templates

A *template* is a PowerPoint 2000 presentation that is used as a model to create other presentations. When you create a new presentation using the AutoContent Wizard, the Wizard automatically selects a template for your presentation. As an alternative, you can select a template yourself when creating a presentation by choosing File⇨New and selecting a template from the Design Templates tab.

If at any time you decide that you don't like the appearance of your presentation, you can change the presentation's look without changing its contents by assigning a new template to the presentation. To do that, follow these steps:

1. Choose Format⇨Apply Design Template.

The Apply Design Template dialog box appears.

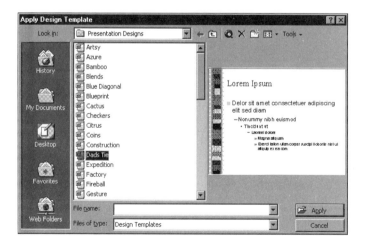

2. Click the template you want to use.

The Preview area shows a preview of each template as you select it.

3. Click the Apply button.

Transitions

A transition is a visual effect that appears when a PowerPoint 2000 slide show moves from one slide to the next. PowerPoint 2000 lets you choose from among many different transition effects, and you can specify a different effect for each slide. In addition, you can easily add sound effects to add even more pizzazz to your presentations. To set the transitions between slides, follow this procedure:

1. Switch to Normal view or Slide Sorter view by choosing View⇨Normal or View⇨Slide Sorter.

2. Select the slide to which you want to add a transition.

Note that the transition always occurs *before* the slide you select. So to set the transition to occur between the first and second slides, select the second slide.

3. Choose Slide Show⇨Slide Transition.

The Slide Transition dialog box appears.

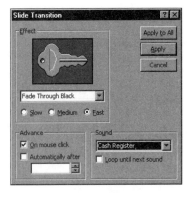

4. Select the transition effect you want from the Effect drop-down list box.

5. Select the speed of the transition by clicking the Slow, Medium, or Fast radio buttons. (Fast is almost always best.)

6. Choose a sound to accompany the transition from the Sound drop-down box.

7. If you want the slide show to run itself automatically, check the Automatically after check box and then enter the number of seconds you want the slide to be displayed. If you want to control the pace of the slide show, check the On mouse click check box.

8. Click the <u>A</u>pply button or press Enter.

For more information, see Chapter 16 of *PowerPoint 2000 For Windows For Dummies.*

Viewer

You can transfer a PowerPoint 2000 presentation to a diskette, from which you can run the presentation on any computer running Windows 95 or 98, by using a special program called the PowerPoint 2000 Viewer. The following sections present the procedures for using the Viewer.

Using the Pack and Go Wizard

To prepare a presentation for use with the PowerPoint 2000 Viewer, use the Pack and Go Wizard. Here's the procedure:

1. Open the presentation you want to copy to diskette.

2. Choose <u>F</u>ile⇨Pac<u>k</u> and Go.

The Pack and Go Wizard appears.

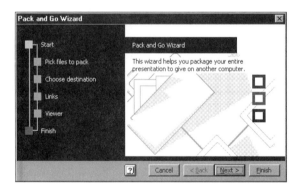

3. Click <u>N</u>ext.

The Wizard asks which presentation you want to include. You can choose between the presentation you have open (Active presentation), another presentation (Other presentation), or both. If you choose Other presentation, the Browse feature activates, which allows you to locate the other presentation on your system.

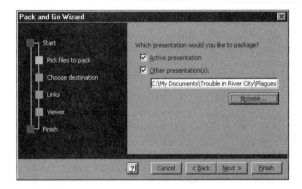

4. Click Next.

The Wizard asks whether you want to copy the presentation to drive A or to a different drive.

5. Change the drive letter if necessary and then click Next.

The Wizard now asks whether you want to Include Linked Files and Embed TrueType fonts. It's usually a good idea to check both options.

6. Click Next again.

The Wizard asks whether you want to include the PowerPoint 2000 Viewer.

It's best to include the Viewer, just in case the computer you want to run the presentation on doesn't have PowerPoint 2000 installed.

7. Click Next.

The Wizard's last screen appears.

8. Insert a diskette in the diskette drive.

9. Click the Finish button.

Copying a packed presentation onto another computer

You can't run a presentation directly from the disk created by the Pack and Go Wizard. Instead, you must first copy the presentation from the diskette to another computer's hard drive by following these steps:

1. Insert the diskette that contains the packed presentation into the disk drive on the computer from which you want to run the presentation.

2. Open the My Computer window by double-clicking its icon and then select the diskette drive into which you inserted the diskette.

3. Double-click the Pngsetup icon to run the Pack and Go Setup program.

4. Follow the instructions that appear on-screen.

Running a slide show by using the Viewer

After you copy the presentation to the other computer, you can run it with the Viewer by following this procedure:

1. Start the PowerPoint 2000 Viewer by double-clicking its icon in the folder into which you copied the presentation.

The system extracts the Viewer onto your hard drive, and the program asks whether you want to run the slide show at this time.

2. Click Yes.

Your slide show starts automatically.

Part VI

Access 2000

Access 2000 is the powerful database program that comes with Microsoft Office 2000 Professional. Because the Standard Edition of Office 2000 does not include Access 2000, you can skip this part if you don't have Office 2000 Professional.

Although Access 2000 is a powerful database program that computer programmers use to create sophisticated applications, you don't need a Ph.D. in computer science to use Access 2000. By using the information in this part, you can create simple databases, design custom forms and reports, and query your database to extract important information. For more information about Access 2000, pick up a copy of *Access 2000 For Windows For Dummies,* by John Kaufeld, published by IDG Books Worldwide, Inc.

In this part . . .

- ✔ **Adding a field to an existing table**
- ✔ **Using the Form Wizard**
- ✔ **Creating a new database**
- ✔ **Entering and editing data**
- ✔ **Creating a query**
- ✔ **Creating a report**

Data

After you create a database, you can enter data into it. The exact procedures you must follow vary, depending on the database, but here is a general procedure you can use:

1. From the Main Switchboard for the database, select one of the options that allows you to enter data.

For example, the following figure shows the Main Switchboard for a Contact Management database. The first two items on this switchboard let you enter data.

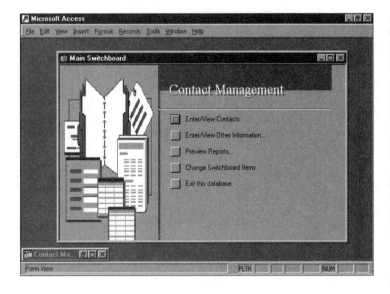

Selecting the first option on this switchboard brings up the following data entry form:

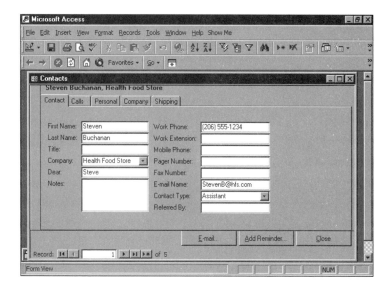

2. Type the information for each field, using the Tab key to move from field to field.

 3. When you have entered all the information for one record, click the New Record button to create the record.

You can then enter data for another record.

4. After you finish entering data, click the form's Close button (the X in the top-right corner) to dismiss the form.

You can change data in an existing record by using one of the navigation buttons that appear at the bottom of the form to display the record. Then, use the Tab key to move to the field you want to change, type a new value into the field, and press Enter. The navigation buttons are described in the following table:

Navigation Button	What It Does
⏮	Displays the first record in the database.
◀	Goes back one record.
▶	Goes forward one record.
⏭	Displays the last record in the database.

To delete a record, use the navigation buttons to call up the record you want to delete and then choose Edit⇨Delete Record. A dialog box appears, warning you that you are about to delete information and that it won't be retrievable. If you really want to delete the record, click the Yes button.

Fields

After you create a database, adding additional fields to any of its tables is a simple matter. Follow these steps to create a new field by using a field in one of the sample tables as a model:

1. If the database's Switchboard is open, close the window by clicking its Close button (located in the upper-right corner, marked by an X) and then open the minimized Database window, as shown in the following figure.

(The Switchboard is a menu that lets you access common database functions, such as entering data or printing reports. The databases created by the Access 2000 database templates all include Switchboards.)

On the left side of the Database screen is a row of buttons labeled Objects.

2. Click the Tables button to access its options; then click the table to which you want to add a field and click the Design button.

The Table window appears, as shown in the following figure:

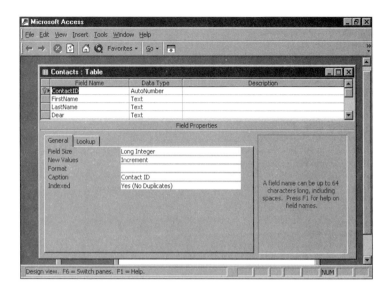

3. Click the row in which you want to insert the new field.

To insert the new field after the existing fields, click the first blank row.

 If you click an already-formatted field and follow these instructions, that field is replaced by the new one that you choose. If you want to add a field without removing any of the old ones, you must first insert a field by clicking the Insert Rows button. Clicking this button inserts a new field immediately before the field that you currently have highlighted.

 4. Click the Build button on the Standard toolbar.

The Field Builder dialog box appears, as shown in the following figure:

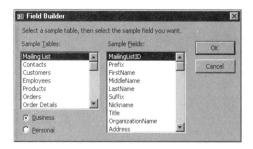

5. Select from the Sample Tables list the sample table that contains the field you want to add and then select the field from the Sample Fields list.

6. Click OK.

Access 2000 adds the field to the table and closes the dialog box.

7. Click the Close button in the upper-right corner of the table design window.

8. Access 2000 asks whether you want to save changes to the table design; click the Yes button.

If you prefer to define the field manually or if no similar field exists in any of the sample databases, follow Steps 1 and 2 of the preceding set of steps and then follow these steps:

1. To insert the new field after the existing fields, click the first blank row.

 To insert the new field among the existing fields, click where you want to insert the new field and then click the Insert Row button on the toolbar.

2. Type the name of the new field in the Field Name column.

3. Click in the Data Type column of that field.

An arrow appears on the right side of the column.

4. Click the arrow to see a drop-down list of field types.

5. Select the field type you want to use for this field.

6. Adjust the properties for the field as necessary, using the properties list that appears at the bottom of the Table window. To change one of the property settings, click the property and type a new value.

7. Click the Close button in the upper-right corner of the Table window to dismiss the window.

8. After Access 2000 asks whether you want to save changes to the table design, click the Yes button.

Form Wizard

One of the best features of Access 2000 is that the program enables you to create custom-designed forms to enter data into or retrieve data from your database. You could spend hours creating forms from scratch. Or you can create a basic form in minutes by using the Form Wizard. To use the Wizard, just follow these steps:

1. Choose File➪Open to open the database for which you want
to create a form, click the Forms tab in the Database window,
and then click the New button.

The New Form dialog box appears, as shown in the following
figure:

2. Select Form Wizard from the list of form types and select a
table or query from the drop-down list. Then click OK.

The Form Wizard appears, as shown in the following figure:

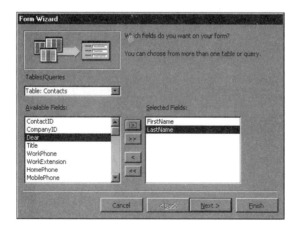

3. Select the fields that you want to include on the form.

To select the fields, first select from the Tables/Queries list
the table that contains the field you want to include on the
form. In the Available Fields list, click the field that you want
to include and then click the > button. Access 2000 removes
the field you select from the Available Fields list and inserts
the field in the Selected Fields list. Repeat this step for each
field you want to include.

4. After you select all the fields that you want to include, click the <u>N</u>ext button.

The Form Wizard dialog box asks how you want the fields arranged on the form, as shown in the following figure:

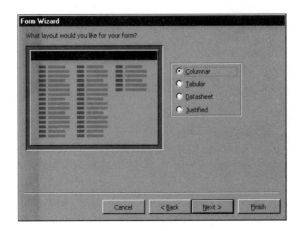

5. Select the radio button for the field layout that you want.

You have the following four choices of form layouts:

- **<u>C</u>olumnar:** The fields are arranged in a column, with one record shown on each form.

- **<u>T</u>abular:** The fields are arranged in a tabular form, with one row of fields for each record. This format displays more than one record at a time.

- **<u>D</u>atasheet:** This layout arranges fields in a spreadsheet-like configuration. This layout also shows more than one record at a time.

- **<u>J</u>ustified:** This layout arranges fields in a grid configuration, adjusting the width of each field so that the table aligns on both the left and right sides. If possible, the Form Wizard places more than one field in each row of the grid. In this layout, only one record is visible at a time.

6. Click the <u>N</u>ext button.

The Form Wizard asks which form style you prefer. These styles provide different background images and text styles.

7. From the list, select the style you prefer and then click the <u>N</u>ext button.

The Form Wizard displays its final screen, as shown in the following figure:

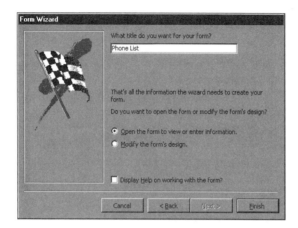

8. Type a title for the form in the text box and then click the Finish button.

The Wizard creates and then displays the form, as shown in the following figure:

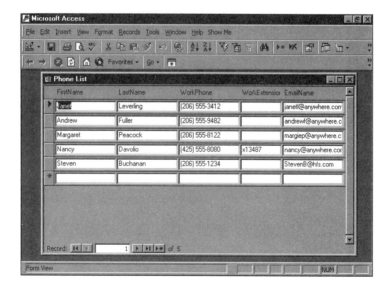

For more information, see *Access 2000 For Windows For Dummies.*

New Database

Creating a database from scratch can be a tedious chore and is best left to database experts. Access 2000, however, comes with a friendly Database Wizard that can perform most of the dirty work for you. All you need to do is answer a few simple questions and enjoy a cup of coffee while the Wizard creates your database fields, forms, and reports. Just follow these steps:

1. Click the Access Database Wizards, Pages, and Projects option button in the dialog box that appears right after you start Access 2000 and then click OK.

The New dialog box appears.

If you already have another database open, close that database by choosing File⇨Close, and then choose File⇨New or click the New button to open the New dialog box.

2. Click the Databases tab of the New dialog box to reveal the list of Database templates, as shown in the following figure:

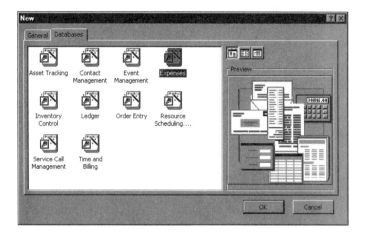

Previous versions of Access included an Address Book database. You may notice that the Database Wizard no longer gives you that option. Instead, it's called "Contact Management." It's the same feature, with a few more features and a more pretentious name.

3. From the list of database templates, click the one that best represents the type of database you want to create.

4. Click OK.

The File New Database dialog box appears, which is basically the same thing as the Open screen showing the directories on your system.

5. Locate and open the folder that you want to use for this database. Type a name for your database in the File Name text box or leave the name that Access 2000 proposes if that name is satisfactory.

6. Click the Create button.

Access 2000 whirs and spins for a moment and then displays the first screen of the Database Wizard, as shown in the following figure:

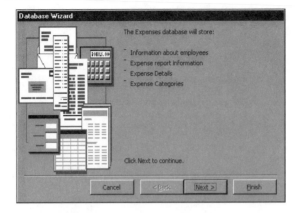

7. Click the <u>N</u>ext button to start the Wizard.

The Wizard proposes certain fields to be included in the database but allows you to select which ones should actually be included, as shown in the following figure:

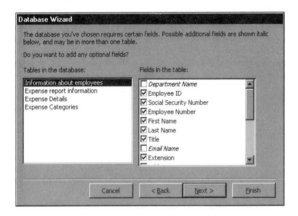

8. Scan the fields in the table list, adding or removing fields from the list of fields proposed for each table by clicking the check box next to the field name.

Note: If the database has more than one table, select the table that you want to examine in the Tables in the Database list box.

9. After you're satisfied with the arrangement of fields for the table, click the <u>N</u>ext button.

The Wizard then asks what style you want it to use for dialog boxes used by the database, as shown in the following figure:

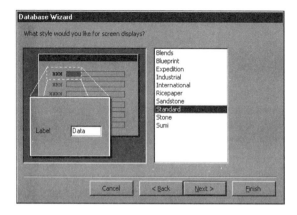

10. Select from the list the display style that suits your fancy and then click the Next button.

The Wizard now asks for your report style preference, which affects such things as the typeface and background colors for your reports, as shown in the following figure:

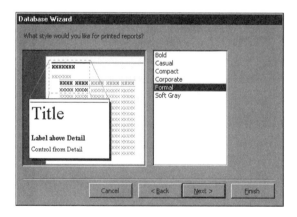

11. Select from the list the report style that pleases you and then click the Next button.

The Wizard asks a few more annoying questions, including what you want to name your database.

12. Type a title for the database in the text box if you are not satisfied with the Wizard's proposed title.

13. If you want to include a picture in all the reports for the database, check the Yes, I'd Like to Include a Picture check box; then click the Picture button and select a picture for the reports.

14. Click the Next button.

The Wizard displays its final screen, which basically tells you that it's done, and you can either start the database or ask for Help to be displayed.

15. Click the Finish button.

Be patient while the Wizard creates the database tables, forms, and reports. After the Wizard finishes, Access 2000 opens the database.

Notice that the Database Wizard creates a Switchboard, which is a menu that's customized for each type of database. To use the Switchboard, just click the buttons that appear next to each option.

To dismiss the Switchboard, click the Switchboard's Close button in the upper-right corner. Then you can open the minimized database window for that database and use the Access 2000 database functions directly.

Queries

A query is the most powerful and difficult-to-use feature of Access 2000. Before you create a query, you need to know the following details:

+ Which tables are involved in the query

+ Which fields you want the query result to show

+ The sequence into which you want the query result sorted

+ Which criteria you want to apply to determine which records Access 2000 selects

Here's the blow-by-blow procedure for creating a query:

1. Open the database for which you want to create a query by choosing File⇨Open. Then click the Queries button on the left side of the Database window and click the New button.

The New Query dialog box appears, as shown in the following figure:

2. Select Simple Query Wizard from the list and then click OK.

The figure shows the dialog box that appears.

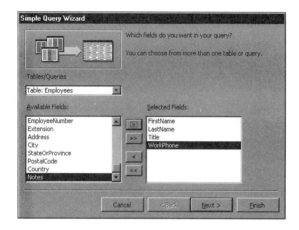

3. Access can take data from more than one table in organizing its queries. In the Tables/Queries drop-down list, select the first table or query that you want to include in your new query.

The fields of that table appear in the Available Fields box.

4. Select each field that you want to include in the query and click the > button.

The field moves from the Available Fields box to the Selected Fields box.

If you want to use the data from more than one table, repeat Steps 3 and 4 until you have all the fields you need for your query.

5. Click the Next button.

What you see next depends on the fields you've selected for your query. If you've chosen all the fields of one table, you can skip to Step 11. However, if your query does not include all the fields from a table or other query, or if you've used fields from more than one table or query, you get something else. In this case, the dialog box that opens gives you the option to view the results of your query either in Detail (showing all the records that match your query results) or as Summary (showing only the calculations of the total records for each field).

6. If you select the Detail option, click the Next button, and then move to Step 11.

If you select the Summary option, you have to click the Summary Options button to answer a few more questions about what you want. The figure shows the Summary Options dialog box.

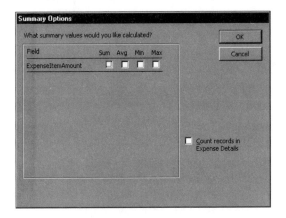

7. The Summary Options dialog box shows the fields in your query that will provide calculations, and you can choose what type of calculations you want for each field.

You are not restricted to choosing only one calculation. You can select any combination, or you can select all of them.

8. When you have selected your options, click OK to return to the Simple Query Wizard.

9. Click Next to proceed to the next step.

10. If you chose the Summary query and your query includes dates, you have one additional dialog box to work through. This one simply wants to know how to organize the date fields you included. Click the radio button that fits your needs and then click Next.

11. The final window of the Simple Query Wizard allows you to give your query a unique name and to either view the results or modify your query design. When you've made your selection, click Finish.

After you save the query, you can run that query at any time by opening the Database window, clicking the Queries tab, and double-clicking the query name in the list of queries. Or, you can just click the query name once and click the Open button.

For more information on queries, see *Access 2000 For Windows For Dummies*.

Reports

Creating a report in Access 2000 is easy if you use the Report Wizards. Report Wizards create various types of reports after asking you questions about the information you want to include. The following procedure shows how to create a simple report showing the purchases made by each customer. The procedure for creating other types of reports is similar.

Here is the procedure for creating a report:

1. Choose File➪Open to open the database for which you want to create a report, click the Reports button on the left side of the Database window, and then click the New button.

The New Report dialog box appears.

2. Select Report Wizard from the list of report types and then click OK.

The Report Wizard appears, as shown in the following figure:

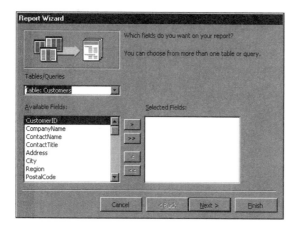

3. Select the fields that you want to include in the report.

To select fields for the report, from the Tables/Queries drop-down list, select the table that contains the fields you want in the report. Then in the Available Fields list, click the field that you want to include and click the > button. Access 2000 removes the field you select from the Available Fields list and inserts that field in the Selected Fields list. Repeat this step for each field that you want to include. In the following figure, I select three fields to include in the report:

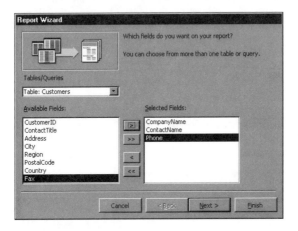

4. After you select all the fields that you want to include, click the Next button.

The Report Wizard dialog box asks its next question, as shown in the following figure:

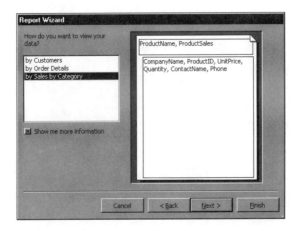

This is what you see if you have selected fields from more than one table or query. (If you've only selected fields from a single source, skip to Step 6.) In this dialog box, the Report Wizard asks you to determine how you want to view your report.

5. Click one of the choices displayed in the window on the left side and see how the organization on the right side changes. After you determine how you want the data organized, click the Next button.

6. The Wizard asks you about the grouping of the report. In the window on the left side, select the first field by which you want to group the report.

The Report Wizard enables you to group the report by up to four fields. You can use the up and down Priority arrows to determine the order of the grouping.

On the lower-left side of this dialog box is a button labeled Grouping Options. This option enables you to determine the grouping intervals for each level of the report. The term *grouping intervals* describes how the items in each category are organized.

In the following figure, I tell the Wizard to sort the report in CompanyName sequence:

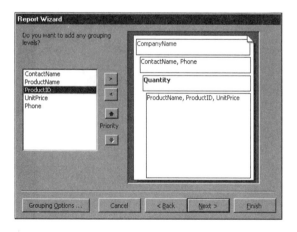

7. After you select the grouping sequence, click the Next button.

The Wizard next asks about the sort order for the grouped items in the report.

8. Select from the first drop-down list the first field by which you want to sort the report.

The Report Wizard enables you to sort the report by up to four fields, and each field can be used to sort the report in ascending or descending sequence.

If you used data from more than one source, the Summary Options button appears in this dialog box. It opens the Summary Options dialog box that allows you to determine how you want your report summarized. You can use it to find the total, the average, the minimum and/or the maximum values of any fields that have numeric values. You can also use this dialog box to show both the details and summary of the report, or just the summary. Click OK when you have set the summary options you want. You return to the Report Wizard.

9. Click the Next button to open the next screen of the Report Wizard.

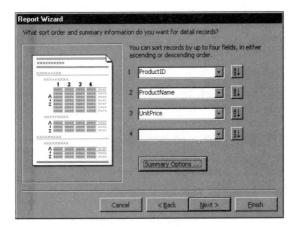

10. You can select the organization of the report on the page: whether it appears as Portrait or Landscape orientation, and whether you want the field widths adjusted automatically so that all fit on the page. When you have determined the layout for your report, click the Next button.

The Wizard then asks you what style to use for the report, as shown in the following figure:

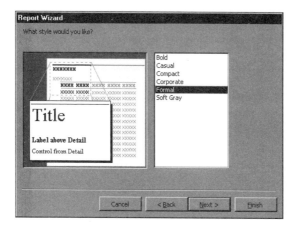

11. Select from the list the report style that suits your fancy and then click the Next button.

The Report Wizard dialog box asks its final question, as shown in the following figure:

12. Change the report title in the text box if you don't like the one that the Wizard proposes, and then click the Finish button.

The Wizard grinds and churns for a few moments while creating the report, and then the Wizard displays the report in preview mode, as shown in the following figure:

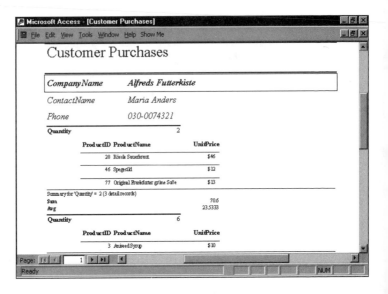

13. To print the report, click the Print button on the Standard toolbar.

14. To save your report design, choose File⇨Save or click the Save button on the toolbar.

Outlook 2000

This part covers Outlook, the all-in-one personal information manager that comes with Microsoft Office 2000. Outlook functions as an address book, a calendar, and a task organizer, and it can even double as your e-mail program. For more information about Outlook 2000, pick up a copy of *Microsoft Outlook 2000 For Dummies,* by Bill Dyszel, published by IDG Books Worldwide, Inc.

In this part . . .

✔ **Creating and maintaining a contact list**

✔ **Tracking appointments and events**

✔ **Sending and receiving e-mail**

✔ **Task management**

Address Book

 Outlook keeps an address book, which allows you to maintain a list of your contacts with addresses, telephone numbers, and other information pertinent to each person. To work with the address book, click the Address Book icon or choose Tools⇨ Address Book. Here is how Outlook appears when you call up your contacts:

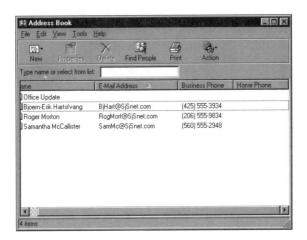

You can use the following procedures to maintain your contact list.

Adding

To add a name to the Outlook address book, follow these steps:

1. Click the New button in the toolbar and select Contact from the drop-down list or select File⇨New⇨Contact from the menu bar.

The Properties window appears, as in the following figure:

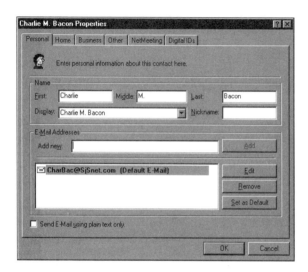

2. In the Personal tab of the dialog box, fill in the contact's name, telephone numbers, addresses, and e-mail address.

The bottom of the box has a window that shows the e-mail addresses of your new contact.

3. The other tabs in this dialog box allow you to make notes regarding the person for future reference, and give you the opportunity to enter a great deal of information that may or may not be useful to you.

4. When you've added all the information you want for your contact, click OK.

Your new contact is displayed in your address book.

You'll also find that you can view your address book by clicking the Contacts button on the left side of the Outlook window. Clicking this button provides you with the opportunity of inputting the same information and viewing it at will, but the format of your data appears differently. You can switch back and forth between using the Address Book version and the Contacts version whenever you want. The same information appears in both versions; it's a matter of which view you find more aesthetically pleasing.

Updating

If the address information or any other information for a contact changes, you can update the contact by following these steps:

1. Switch to the Address Book view by clicking the Address Book button.

2. Double-click the contact you want to change.

The Properties dialog box for that person opens.

3. Enter any changes you want in the various tabs of the Properties dialog box.

4. Click OK.

The Properties dialog box closes and your changes are automatically saved.

Calendar

 One of the main functions of Outlook is keeping a calendar so that you can track appointments and upcoming events. To switch to the Outlook calendar, click the Calendar icon in the Outlook Bar (the Outlook Bar is the list of icons along the left edge of the Outlook window) or choose Go⇨Calendar. The following figure shows what Outlook's calendar looks like:

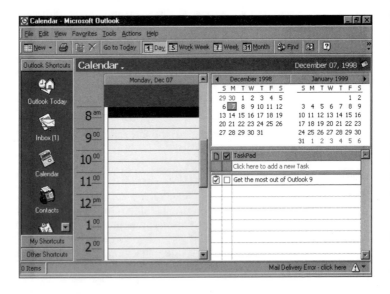

The following sections describe the most common procedures for using the Outlook 2000 calendar.

 After you install Office 2000 on your system, you may notice that there are icons for Microsoft Outlook and for Outlook Express. *They are not the same thing!* This chapter covers Microsoft Outlook.

Cancelling appointments

To cancel an appointment, follow these steps:

1. Highlight the appointment in the calendar you want to cancel to select that appointment.

 2. Click the Delete button.

The appointment disappears from the calendar.

Rescheduling appointments

Here's the procedure for rescheduling an appointment by dragging it to a new time or date:

1. Switch to a calendar view that shows both the appointment you want to reschedule and the date to which you want to reschedule it.

(***See also*** the section "Views" for more information.)

To move an appointment to a different time on the same day, for example, switch to Day view. To reschedule to a different day in the same week, switch to Week view.

2. Click the appointment to select it.

3. Drag the appointment to the new time and/or day.

 You can also reschedule an appointment by double-clicking the appointment to open the Appointment dialog box and then adjusting the Start Time and End Time fields in the dialog box. (If you change the start time, the end time is automatically adjusted to keep the appointment the same length. If you change the end time, the start time is not changed. Instead, the duration of the appointment changes.)

Scheduling recurring appointments

You can use Outlook to schedule recurring appointments, such as staff meetings or other annoying appointments that you hate to go to every day, week, or month. Here's the procedure:

1. Follow the procedure outlined in the section "Creating appointments" later in this part, to create an appointment for the next occurrence of the recurring date.

If you have a staff meeting from 12:00 to 1:30 every Friday afternoon, for example, schedule the appointment for next Friday.

2. Double-click the appointment to open the Appointment window, as shown in the following figure:

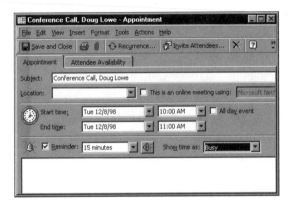

3. Click the Recurrence button to open the Appointment Recurrence dialog box, as shown in the following figure:

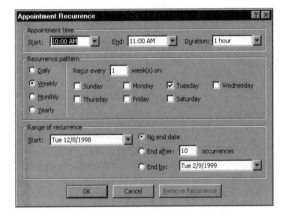

Outlook initially assumes that the appointment occurs every week on the same day and time. If this is not the case (for example, if the appointment should be every other week or monthly), you can make any necessary changes now.

4. If necessary, change the Recurrence Pattern options to indicate the frequency of the appointment (Daily, Weekly, Monthly, or Yearly).

After you change the frequency option, a new set of controls appears in the Recurrence Pattern area of the Appointment Recurrence dialog box, enabling you to specify the exact schedule for the recurring appointment. To schedule an appointment that occurs only on the fourth Friday of every month, for example, you click Monthly. A set of list box controls then appears. These controls enable you to specify that the appointment occurs on a certain day each month — in this case, on the fourth Friday.

5. Click OK and then click the <u>S</u>ave and Close button.

 Outlook adds a special icon to the appointment in the calendar to indicate that the appointment is recurring.

Creating appointments

To create an appointment, follow these steps:

1. Switch to the calendar view in which you prefer to work.

Daily or weekly views are best for scheduling appointments. (***See also*** the section "Views" for more information.)

2. Click the day on which you want to schedule the appointment.

3. Click the time slot during which you want to schedule the appointment.

If you want the appointment to stretch beyond a single time interval, drag the mouse across the desired time periods.

4. Type a description for the appointment.

You're done. The following figure shows a lunch appointment scheduled, shown in Day view:

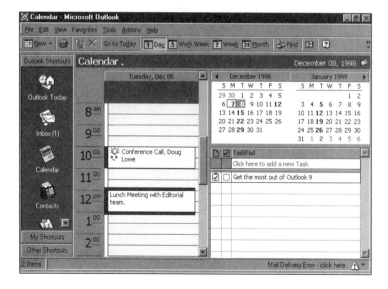

Events

An *event* is an item that occurs on a specific calendar date but does not have a particular time associated with it. Examples of events include birthdays, anniversaries, vacations, and so on.

To add an event to your calendar, follow these steps:

1. Switch to the calendar view in which you want to work — Day, Week, or Month.

(*See also* the section "Views" for details.)

2. In the calendar, click the date on which the event occurs.

3. Select <u>A</u>ctions⇨New All Day <u>E</u>vent from the menu bar.

The Event dialog box appears, as shown in the following figure:

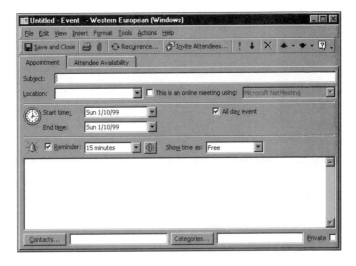

4. Type a description for the event in the Subject box.

5. If the event continues for more than one day, change the ending date by selecting a date from the End Ti<u>m</u>e drop-down list.

6. If it is a reminder of a birthday, anniversary, or some other similar event, make sure there is a check in the All Da<u>y</u> Event check box.

7. The Sho<u>w</u> Time As drop-down list allows you to set to "Free," which reminds you of the date but doesn't block your day from other appointments.

8. If this is a personal matter, make sure the Private check box is marked. This will prevent other people on your network from receiving this message.

9. After you have all the features marked, click the Save and Close button.

The event appears on your calendar.

The following figure shows how a typical event appears in daily calendar view:

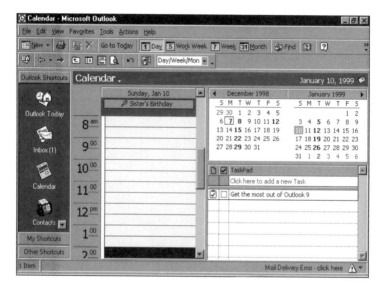

Meetings

If everyone in your office uses Outlook and your computers are connected via a network, you can use the Plan a Meeting feature to schedule meetings electronically. Outlook automatically picks a time slot that's available for each participant and notifies everyone of the time and place of the meeting.

Follow these steps to plan a meeting:

1. Choose Actions⇨Plan a Meeting. The Plan a Meeting dialog box appears, as shown in the following figure:

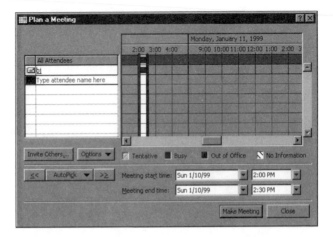

2. Type the names of the people with whom you want to schedule a meeting in the All Attendees column. Or click the Invite Others button to summon the Select Attendees and Resources dialog box. This dialog box lets you select names from your address book. After you select everyone you want to invite, click OK to dismiss the Select Attendees and Resources dialog box.

Outlook reviews each person's schedule so that you can see who has free time (and when).

3. Pick a time when everyone is free by clicking the time in the schedule area of the Appointment dialog box. Or click AutoPick to have Outlook pick the time for you.

4. Click the Make Meeting button.

Outlook displays the following window:

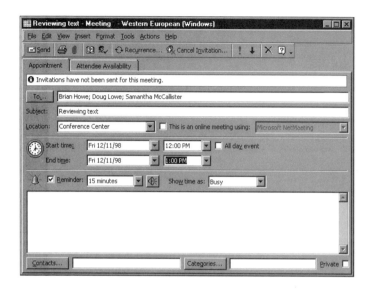

5. Type a subject for the meeting invitation in the Subject box and a location in the Location box.

6. Click the Send button in the window's toolbar to send the invitations.

If someone invites you to a meeting, you receive an e-mail message that includes three buttons you can click to reply to the invitation: Accept, Decline, or Tentative. Click the appropriate button to reply to the invitation.

Views

Outlook gives you four calendar views: Day, Work Week, Week, and Month. To change views, click the following buttons in the toolbar:

 ✦ Day

 ✦ Work Week

 ✦ Week

 ✦ Month

The Outlook calendar also enables you to view active appointments, scheduled events, annual events, and recurring appointments. You can see these views via the drop-down list that appears when you choose View➪Current View.

E-Mail

Outlook includes an integrated e-mail feature that can send and receive electronic mail from your various e-mail services. If you receive e-mail from your local area network, from the Internet, or from the Microsoft Network, Outlook can read e-mail from all three sources. That way, you don't need to fuss around with three separate e-mail programs.

 To access the Outlook e-mail feature, click the Inbox icon. The following figure shows the Inbox:

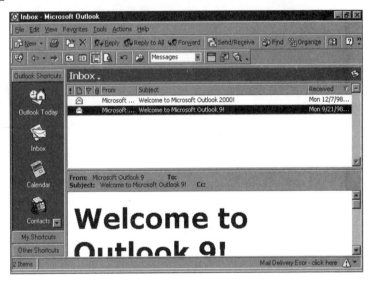

The following sections describe how to accomplish the most important tasks in using Outlook e-mail.

Reading e-mail

Reading e-mail is easy in Outlook. All you do is double-click the message you want to read in the Inbox. The message appears in its own window, as shown in the following figure:

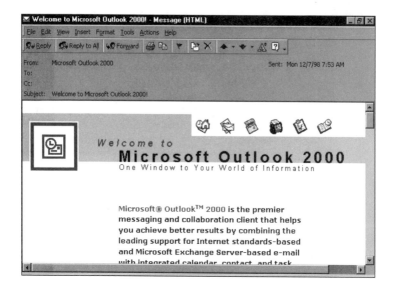

After you finish reading the message, close the window by clicking the Close button (the button with the X in the upper-right corner of the window). Or click any of the buttons described in the following list to respond to the message or to read other messages:

✦ Clicking the Previous Item button opens a drop-down list that allows you to look at previous e-mail from any one of a number of categories. Outlook allows you to sort your e-mail into different folders by topic, to flag the message as important, or to organize your e-mail by topic. Use this drop-down list to select which earlier piece of e-mail you want to read.

✦ Clicking the Next Item button also opens a drop-down list that allows you to select any item in your e-mail queue that fits the category you select.

✦ Clicking this button replies to everyone on the previous message's e-mail list.

✦ Clicking this button forwards the message to another recipient.

✦ Use this button to put a flag that appears next to the message in the In Box. This feature allows you to see the message at a glance so that you remember to follow it up.

✦ Clicking the Move to Folder button allows you to save your e-mail to a folder that you determine or to Outlook's calendar feature.

✦ Click this button to delete the message.

Replying to e-mail

To reply to an e-mail message, follow these steps:

1. Click the Reply button to open the window shown in the following figure:

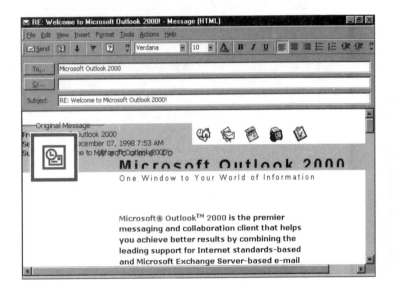

2. Type your response.

Outlook automatically displays the contents of the original message below your response. You can delete as much of the original message as you want by selecting the text and pressing the Delete key.

3. Click the Send button.

Sending e-mail

To send a new e-mail message, follow these steps:

1. Click the New Mail button to make the dialog box shown in the following figure appear:

2. In the To text box, type the e-mail address of the recipient (or recipients). If you want to pick names from your Address Book, click the To button. A dialog box listing all your

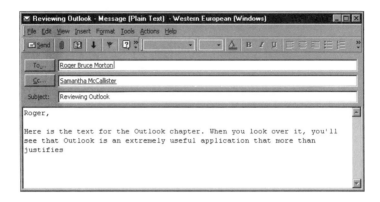

contacts who have e-mail addresses appears; select the recipient you want and then click OK.

3. Type the e-mail address of anyone you want to receive a courtesy copy of the message in the Cc... field. To pick names from your Address Book, click the Cc... button.

4. Type the subject of your message in the Subject text box.

5. Type the body of your message in the message area, the large text box at the bottom of the Message dialog box.

 6. Click the Send button in the toolbar.

 To attach a file to your message, click the Insert File button to bring up an Insert File dialog box (which, unsurprisingly, looks just like the Open dialog box). Select the file you want to attach from this dialog box and then click OK.

Tasks

Outlook enables you to keep a task list, which is a constant reminder that you have miles to go before you sleep . . . and miles to go before you sleep. The following figure shows the Outlook task list:

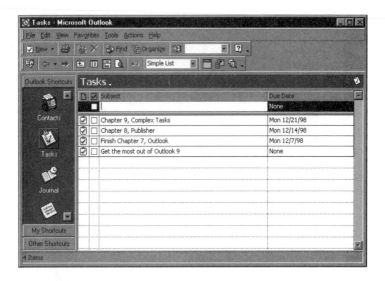

Creating a task

To add an item to your task list, follow these steps:

1. Click the New button.

The New Task dialog box opens.

2. Fill in the New Task dialog box with the details of the task you want to complete.

The New Task dialog box has two tabs. The Task tab allows you to fill in the general information about that task. This is what appears on the Task List. The Details tab allows you to keep a record of the work you do on the task. This tab is helpful for billing companies for your work.

3. After you have the task entered, click the Save and Close button.

The task is then added to the top of the Task List.

Sigh. You have so much to do.

Task requests

Outlook allows you to create a task and then give it to someone else on your network. This is useful for distributing job assignments to subordinates or team members. One thing to always keep in mind is that as soon as you assign a task to another person, as far as Outlook is concerned, you give up ownership of the task. You can keep it in your Task List and receive updates from the person performing the task, but you can't change any of the information regarding the task. Only the person doing the work can do that.

To use Outlook to assign a task to another person:

1. Open the Task List by clicking the Task button on the left side of the Outlook window.

2. Click the arrow next to the New button on the toolbar to open the New Task drop-down list. Select Task Request from this list.

The Task Request window opens, as shown here:

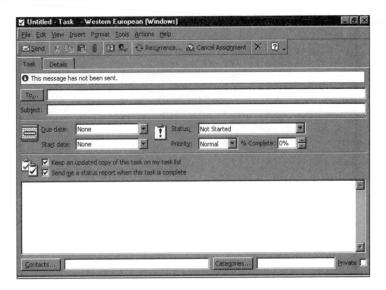

Notice that this looks like a cross between the New Task dialog box and the Send E-mail dialog box.

3. Enter the e-mail address of the person who you're assigning to the job in the To text box, or click the To button to see your address book. Enter the assignment in the Subject window and complete the Due date and Start date list boxes. Determine the Priority of the task and its Status.

4. Put a check in the Keep an Updated Copy of This Task on My Task List check box if you want to track the other person's progress on this assignment. If you want to know when the task is finished, put a check in the Send Me a Status Report When This Task Is Complete check box.

5. You can control your task request even further. You can attach a file to the request by clicking the Insert File button.

Designate the task as regularly recurring by using the Recurrence button.

6. You can enter any explanatory text in the window at the bottom of this window.

Treat this just like a normal e-mail message

7. Click the Send button, and the other person receives your request.

Outlook gives the other person the option of accepting or rejecting the assignment (even if you don't). After the person accepts or rejects the task request, Outlook automatically notifies you via e-mail.

Part VIII

Publisher 2000

Publisher is Microsoft's powerful desktop publishing application that allows you to create professional-looking documents suitable for publication. Publisher is different from other desktop publishing tools, because it allows you to produce striking results without any special training (or even any particular artistic skill). One of the nicest features of Publisher is that it is fully integrated with the other Office programs and uses most of the same conventions and tools as Word 2000. For more information about Publisher 2000 and how to use it, please look at Part VII of *Office 2000 For Dummies,* by Wally Wang and Roger Parker (IDG Books Worldwide, Inc.).

In this part . . .

- ✔ **Importing text from other applications**
- ✔ **Inserting graphics into your document**
- ✔ **Layering text and images in your document**
- ✔ **Formatting your Publisher documents**
- ✔ **Moving graphics around in your document**
- ✔ **Working with the Publisher Wizards**
- ✔ **Using the Pack and Go Wizard**
- ✔ **Using Personal Profiles to speed up your work**

Arranging Objects on a Page

One of the most difficult things about working with different objects is making sure that everything lines up neatly. Publisher takes care of this for you, so you don't have to worry about having a steady hand and precise mouse control.

To have Publisher arrange the objects in your document:

1. Click the object you want to have aligned.

If you want to align more than one object at once, hold down the Shift key before clicking the objects, and then click each object you want to have Publisher move.

2. Select Arrange⇨Align Objects.

The Align Objects dialog box opens.

3. Make selections in the dialog box.

This dialog box has two sets of four radio buttons. The first set of buttons, Left to right, lets you determine whether the object is aligned on the left side of the page, the right side, to the center, or left unchanged on this axis. Click the radio button you want for the horizontal alignment of this frame.

The second set of radio buttons, Top to bottom, gives you control over whether the object is moved to the top of the page, the bottom of the page, positioned in the center, or left unchanged on the vertical axis. Click the radio button you want for the vertical alignment of the frame.

If you want the object to be aligned flush with the page margin, make sure that the Align Along Margins check box is marked.

4. Click OK.

Publisher moves the object to the location you gave it. Unfortunately, it doesn't move any other object that may also be in that space; you have to move that yourself. Fortunately, you can follow the same procedure.

Autoflow

Each of the text frames of a template gives you an idea of how many words it can hold. This can be changed by adjusting the size of the frame, but sometimes (especially if you're putting together a newsletter) your text is simply too large for the space where you want to put it. Don't worry! Publisher has a tool called Autoflow to help you out in this situation. To work with Autoflow, follow these simple steps:

1. Copy and paste the text into the text frame where you want the text to first appear.

If the text is too large, a dialog box appears that says, "The inserted text doesn't fit in this frame. Do you want to use Autoflow?"

2. Click Yes.

Publisher jumps to the next text frame and asks if you want the autoflow to continue to that frame.

Now you have to make some choices that depend on the type of document you're building and the amount of material you still have to add. If, for example, you're laying out a newsletter, you may want to have several articles start on the first page, with autoflow running to other pages later in the document.

3. In most cases, click No.

Autoflow jumps to the next available text frame and asks you the same question. It keeps doing this until all the text has found a home in the document.

If you don't mind text frames that are close together, click Yes in this step. You can keep repeating this until all the text is inserted into the document.

Designing Graphic Objects

Publisher's Design Gallery gives you the opportunity to create your own designs for use in your publications. It does this by providing you with a series of templates that you can customize to fit your taste and needs. You can open the Design Gallery from any Publisher document and use that design in that document. Publisher saves that design so that you can use it again and again.

 To work with the Design Gallery, follow these steps:

1. Open the document where you want to create the new design.

2. Click the Design Gallery Object button, or select Insert⇨ Design Gallery Object located on the bottom of the toolbar that runs along the left side of the Publisher window.

The Publisher Design Gallery opens.

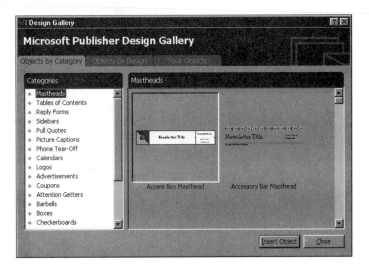

The Design Gallery has three tabs: Objects by Category, Objects by Design, and Your Objects. You can use the Your Objects tab after you've created one or more design objects; they appear on this tab so you can insert them into future documents.

The Objects by Category tab allows you to pick the type of object that you want to make. You can choose to make a masthead, letterhead, logo, marquee, or any other design element of a publication. In the window to the right, you see samples of the object type using different design features.

The Objects by Design tab gives you the opportunity to pick a specific design feature, such as ovals, arcs, or crossed lines. The window to the right then shows you samples of the design element used with different object types.

3. Click the design template you've chosen to work with.

For this set of steps, I've decided to create a logo and have chosen the Open Oval template to be used on the return address of an envelope.

4. Click the Insert Object button.

The design object is inserted onto your document.

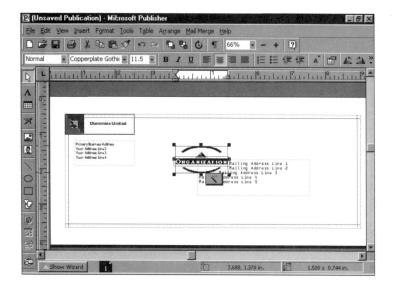

 Occasionally, the Design Wizard button doesn't appear when you insert a design object. If you encounter this, don't worry. It simply means that, except for resizing, you can't modify the object any further.

 5. When you insert the design object into the document, a Wizard button appears at the lower edge of the object and appears anytime you are working with that frame. If you click it, the Design Creation Wizard opens and gives you the option of further modifying the object.

The Design Creation Wizard has four areas you can change.

✦ The New or Existing option allows you to tell the Wizard that you want to include your own graphic to the design object. It has two radio buttons. If you click Picture File That I Already Have, the design changes to a circle with a camera in it. This acts as a placeholder for you to substitute your own graphic file.

✦ Sometimes you may choose a design feature in the Design Gallery only to find that it doesn't work in the document. You can use the Design option of the Wizard to change the design of your object. Any of the choices from the Objects by Design tab of the Design Gallery are available with this option.

✦ The Graphic option lets you tell the Wizard whether you want to insert a graphic file in the design object. If you do, click the Yes button. If not, click No.

✦ Finally, the Number of Lines option lets you determine how many lines of text are available in the design object. Choose the option that you think will work; if you change your mind, you can always return to the Wizard and change this option.

6. At this stage, you most likely have to remove one or more frames from your document to make room for your new design object. After you do, you can move and resize the design object to fit the available space.

7. If you want to include a graphic file as part of your design object, click the graphic frame included in the design object.

It's best if you take a second to press the Delete button to remove the placeholder graphic that is there. You can then insert a graphic file using the method described in "Graphics", later in this part.

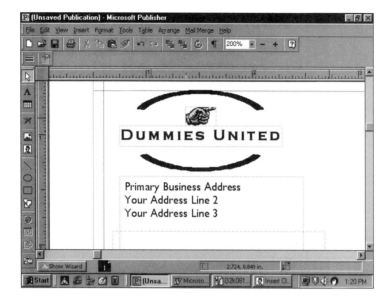

8. If you want to save your design for use in future documents, highlight it and select Insert⇨Add Selection to Design Gallery.

You find your design on the Your Objects tab of the Design Gallery.

Editing Text

You can edit your text in Publisher, but I don't recommend it. Publisher is happiest when it can think of each frame as a single object; when you start editing the text inside a frame, you're making it think about smaller things than it would like. A better approach is to take care of all your editing tasks in Word, before you import your text to Publisher. With that said, there are times when you may discover that you need to make last-minute changes to your text. No, you don't have to go back to the original Word file and start all over — here's how you can take care of the matter:

1. Right-click anywhere inside the text frame you need to edit.

2. Select Change Text.

The pop-up list shown here opens.

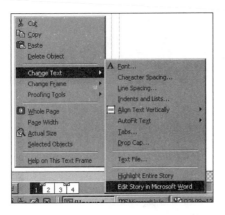

3. Notice that at the bottom of the list is Edit Story in Microsoft Word. If you click this, Word opens with the text you need to edit.

4. Go ahead and make any changes you want.

5. When you're finished, click the Save button.

You won't actually be saving the Word document, but you will transfer all your changes to the Publisher document.

Formatting Your Publisher Documents

The Publisher Format menu changes depending on if you have a text frame or a graphic frame selected. Although it is to your advantage to take care of as much formatting and editing of your text and graphics in their source applications, there is formatting that you need to do after the objects are inserted into the Publisher document. The following sections serve as a brief run-down of the formatting choices you need to make.

Formatting graphic objects

Formatting Command	What It Does
Recolor Picture	Opens a dialog box that gives you the choice of changing the color of the graphic. You have the option of selecting only one color, but your graphic will contain different shades of that color so that the loss of detail is minimized. This is most useful for line-drawings and other single-color images, but it can also be used to make a multi-colored image suitable for single-color printing.

Formatting Command	What It Does
Scale Picture	Opens a dialog box that lets you increase or decrease the height and width of the graphic by a percentage of the current size. To make the image smaller, use numbers under 100. To make the image bigger, use numbers over 100.
Crop Picture	When you select this command, your cursor changes to a crop icon whenever it's positioned over the corner of the graphic frame. Click and drag on the frame's corner with this cursor to make the frame larger or smaller without changing the size of the image.
Fill Color	Opens a dialog box that lets you choose a color for the background of the graphic image. The image itself isn't changed, but the color of the empty space inside the frame is. This command also appears on the Text Formatting menu.
Line/Border Style	Lets you determine the width of the line that forms the border around a graphic frame, including not having a border at all. Also appears on the Text Formatting menu.
Shadow	Creates a shadowed effect in your graphic image. Doesn't work for every image (especially line drawings), so make sure it will work for the images you've selected before you depend on it. Also appears on the Text Formatting menu.
Size and Position	Opens a dialog box that gives you your greatest control over the size and positioning of the graphic frame. This lets you determine (to 1/100th of an inch) the exact size of your graphic and its placement on the page. Also used on the Text Formatting menu.
Picture Frame Properties	Opens a dialog box that lets you determine how the wrap-around feature works (whether text will wrap around the whole frame or just the image in the frame). Also gives you control over the width margins inside the frame.
Color Scheme	This command lets you adjust the color scheme of the entire document, not just the frame that's selected. It opens the Color Scheme dialog box (exactly as what you see in the Publisher Wizard whenever you create a new document) where you can choose the overall scheme for the document. This command also appears on the Text Formatting menu.
Pick Up Formatting	This command also appears on the Text Formatting menu. If you highlight a frame and click this command, the formatting information is copied and stored for later use.

(continued)

Formatting Command	What It Does
Apply Formatting	After you have used the Pick Up Formatting command, you can click another frame and use Apply Formatting to change the format of the new frame to match the frame which you used Pick Up Formatting on. Also appears on the Text Formatting menu.

Formatting text objects

Formatting Command	What It Does
Font	Opens the Font dialog box. This is almost identical to the Font dialog box you see in Word, and is used the same way.
Character Spacing	This command opens the Character Spacing dialog box, which is a very important feature for any desktop publishing. This dialog box allows you to control the width of the characters in the selected frame, as well as the space between the characters. This helps you control how much space any particular body of text takes up in your document.
Line Spacing	This command opens the Line Spacing dialog box, which allows you to control how many points of space are permitted between lines of text.
Indents and Lists	The Indents and Lists dialog box gives you control over how the highlighted text frame is indented. You can control the justification, size of indents, and automatically turn text into bulleted or numbered lists.
Drop Cap	Opens the Drop Caps dialog box so you can determine whether or not you want the first letter of each paragraph to have a dropped cap (that is, a cap that is much larger than the rest of the text). It also gives you a selection of seven different styles of dropped caps.
Align Text Vertically	Gives you the choice of aligning the text in the highlighted frame to the top, the bottom, or in the center of the frame.
AutoFit Text	This highly useful feature lets you tell Publisher that you want to try to force a body of text to fit into the designated frame. You can choose None (and use the Autoflow feature if all the text doesn't fit the frame), Best Fit (and Publisher does its best to format the text to fit in the available frame), or Shrink Text On Overflow (which decreases the size and tighten the character spacing of any text that has to overflow to another frame).

Formatting Command	What It Does
Text Frame Properties	The Text Frame Properties dialog box lets you determine the margin width inside the text frame. It also gives you command over the number of columns in the text frame, whether or not you use wraparound, and lets you use "continued" messages on Autoflow.
Text Style	This opens a series of dialog boxes that, if you work through them allows you to apply a different format to the highlighted text frame. This includes what Word considers to be both Font and Paragraph formatting. I'm not sure why this command also appears on the Graphic Formatting menu, but it does.

Frames

When you open a document template, each frame (whether for text or for graphics) is given a specific purpose and a particular size, depending upon the established purpose for that frame.

Adjusting the size

You don't have to stick with what the designers at Microsoft think is best for you — you can change the size of any frame to adjust for larger or smaller objects than it was initially designed for. This is a simple procedure; just follow these steps.

1. Each frame has a thin-lined box around it. Click once with the left mouse button inside the box.

A series of eight black squares (called *selection handles*) appear around the box.

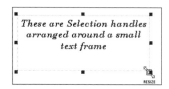

These are Selection handles arranged around a small text frame

RESIZE

2. Move your cursor to the selection handle that is on the side you want to adjust.

The cursor icon changes to the resize icon.

3. Click with the left mouse button and drag the cursor in the direction you want the frame to change. When you have it the size you want on that side, release the mouse button.

4. Repeat as needed on the other sides of the frame until it is the size and shape you want.

Deleting

If the Publisher template you are working with has a frame (whether text or graphic) that you don't want in your document, you can remove it quickly and easily. Here's how:

1. Locate the frame you want to remove and right-click it.

2. Select <u>D</u>elete Object from the drop-down list that appears.

Grouping and ungrouping

Many of the Publisher templates have a group/ungroup feature that binds two or more frames together so that they can be manipulated as a single object. This is most frequently used to group a graphic frame with a text frame (to give the graphic a caption), but can be used anytime you want to keep two or more frames together and to work with them as a single object. But, as usual, you are given a choice over whether or not you want this feature.

To group two or more frames together:

1. Hold down the Shift key and click with the mouse on each frame you want in the group. Don't release the Shift key until you've clicked all the frames you're including.

 2. At the bottom of the frames you've just clicked, you see a Group Objects button. Click this, and your frames are now locked together.

To ungroup two or more frames:

1. Click any one of the grouped frames.

The Ungroup Objects button appears at the bottom of the lowest frame.

 2. Click the Ungroup Objects button.

Moving

Most of the templates in Publisher have pre-set locations for their frames, whether they are text or graphic. This doesn't mean that you have to stick with what the template gives you. You can move a frame from one location in the document to any other. This is very simply done; just follow these steps.

1. Each frame has a thin-lined box around it. Position your cursor along one of the edges of the box. When you do this, a cute little icon of a moving truck appears at your cursor position. Click once with the left mouse button.

A series of eight black squares (called *selection handles*) appear around the box.

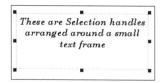

These are Selection handles arranged around a small text frame

2. If you want to move the frame to another location on the same page, skip to Step 3; otherwise, if you want to move the frame to another page, click the Cut button to put the text frame in your Clipboard. Move to the page where you want the frame located, and click the Paste button.

The frame appears on the screen.

3. After you have the frame on the page you want, position the moving cursor over the line of the box *between* the selection handles. Click and drag the text frame to where you want it positioned.

Graphic Frames

You can create a graphic frame and link or embed an image in it very quickly and easily. Here's how:

1. Choose one of the following:

If you want to use one of your own graphics files to link or embed in your Publisher document, click the Picture Frame Tool button.

If you want to embed an image from the Clip Art Gallery, click the Clip Gallery Tool button.

2. Position your cursor at the corner of where you want the graphic frame to be positioned. Click and drag the mouse to the opposite corner. Release the mouse button.

3. Move your cursor to any spot inside the newly-created frame. Double-click the left mouse button.

   If you used the Picture Frame Tool, the Insert Picture window opens. If you used the Clip Gallery Tool, the Clip Art Gallery opens.

4. Locate the image you want to use and link or embed it the same way as described in "Graphics."

Graphics

Publisher treats graphics frames much like text frames; each frame is an object that can be manipulated as a single unit. The big difference between graphics and text files is whether you decide to embed the graphic file or link it to the Publisher document.

Linking the graphic to the document keeps the graphic as a separate file, which you can then work with independent of the rest of the Publisher document. Embedding a graphic makes it an actual part of the Publisher document and it then cannot be treated as a different file. If you intend to send the document to be commercially printed, Microsoft recommends that you link the graphic to the Publisher file rather than embed it. This is because commercial printing houses may need to tinker with the colors and resolution of the graphic before it is finally printed.

Embedding graphics in your document

To embed a graphic image in your Publisher document:

1. Click the frame where you want to embed the graphic.

   If you need to create a frame for this graphic, please *see* "Graphic Frames" earlier in this part.

2. Select Insert⇨Picture.

3. Choose whether to use the Clip Art Gallery or take a graphic from your own files in the drop-down list that appears.

   What you use depends on you.

   You can also import graphics by right-clicking in the target frame and selecting Change Picture⇨Picture from the pop-up list. From there, you can select either Clip Art or From File, depending on the nature of the graphic you want to use.

4. Choose one of the following:

If you have your own graphic file you want to use, click the Erom File option. A browser window opens that allows you to navigate through your system until you find the location of the file you want to include. When you find the file, click it and click the Insert button. The graphic is inserted into your document.

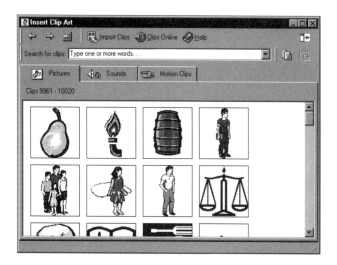

If you are using the Clip Art Gallery, click the Clip Art option. The Clip Art Gallery opens and allows you to choose from over 10,000 different images that are in the public domain. Scroll through the Gallery until you find the image you want and click it. A drop-down list containing four buttons opens. Click the Insert Clip button (the top button of the four), and the image is transferred to your document.

When you insert a graphic file into a frame, the graphic image adjusts to fit the size of the frame. However, if the proportion (the length of the sides compared to the length of the top and bottom) of the graphic is different than that of the frame, the frame shifts to the proportion of the graphic, and the adjoining frames automatically adjust to make up the difference.

Linking graphics to your document

Linking a graphic to a Publisher document is similar to the steps for embedding a graphic; however, there are some slight, but significant, differences.

To link a graphic to a Publisher document:

1. Click the frame where you want to link the graphic.

If you need to create a frame for this graphic, please **see** "Graphic Frames" earlier in this part.

2. Select Insert⇨Picture⇨From File.

Publisher is not set up to link images from its Clip Art Gallery to your Publisher document. Unless you want to go through a lot of hassle of locating the clip art files, you can only link your own graphic files. This is okay, though. Theoretically, all the clip art files have already been adjusted for commercial publication and can be embedded rather than linked without a problem later on.

3. Locate the graphic file you want to use, click it, and then click the arrow to the right of the Insert button.

A drop-down list appears.

4. Click Link to File.

A lower resolution image of the graphic appears in your document, and a link is created to the original graphic file so that any changes that are made to it are reflected in the Publisher document.

Importing Text from Other Applications

It is possible to use Publisher as a word processor and type your text directly into the Publisher document. However, this is cumbersome. It's sort of like using a screwdriver to pound in a nail — it will get the job done, but it's not the best tool you could use. A better approach would be to type your text in a Word document and then import it to the Publisher document.

Publisher prefers to work with already completed blocks of text that have been tweaked and fussed over using another, more appropriate, application. After the text is ready, you can insert it into something that Publisher calls a *text frame*, which you can then work with as a single object.

To do this:

1. Open Word and enter the text you want. Make sure to save your work as you go.

It's worth your while to do all your editing of the document while you're still in Word.

2. Highlight all the text you want to import and click the Copy button, or use Edit⇨Copy.

This saves the text in the Clipboard.

3. Open the Publisher document, locate the text frame where you want to place the text and press Ctrl+A.

This highlights all the placeholder text currently in that location. You can also highlight the text by triple-clicking the left mouse button.

 If you've been working in Publisher and want to use Word documents that you've previously entered, you don't have to go through the tiresome business of opening Word and locating that file. Instead, right-click the frame where you want to import a new text file. Select Change Text⇨Text File. This opens an Explorer window that allows you to locate the file you need. Double-click that filename, and it's automatically imported into your Publisher document, in the frame you've indicated.

4. Press the Delete key.

You need to get rid of the filler text before copying your new material, otherwise some of it may be attached at the end of your own work.

5. Click the Paste button, or select Edit⇨Paste.

Voilà! You're done! Well, almost. There are some situations that require a little more thought on your part, especially if the text you've chosen to move is larger than the area you've given it. If this happens, there are several options available to you. ***See*** "Autoflow."

Layering Objects in Your Documents

This is where we start getting fancy with creating Publisher documents. You can *layer* the frames on your document, so that two frames occupy the same space and can both be seen by your reader. This is how you create backgrounds, headers and footers, specially designed borders, or watermarks.

Layering objects on a single page

If you just want to layer an object on a single page of your document, follow these steps.

1. Open your document to the page where you want the background to appear.

2. Insert the object onto the page (*see* "Importing Text from Other Applications" or "Graphics").

3. Adjust the size and position of the object to where you want it (*see* "Moving," or "Adjusting the size").

 4. Click the Send to Back button, or select Arrange⇨Send to Back.

The object disappears behind the other objects on the page.

 5. If you want to see or work with the background object, simply click the Bring to Front button, or select Arrange⇨Bring to Front.

Layering objects on every page of a document

Watermarks, headers and footers appear on every page of a document. It's easy to do this:

1. With your document open, select View⇨Go to Background.

An apparently blank page appears.

2. Insert the object onto the page (*see* "Importing Text from Other Applications" or "Graphics").

3. Adjust the size and position of the object to where you want it (*see* "Moving").

4. Select View⇨Go to Foreground.

The background disappears, to be replaced with the foreground objects in your document.

Pack and Go Wizard

The Pack and Go Wizard is a wonderful new feature to Publisher 2000. It allows you to pack up your Publisher document with all of the associated linked files and send it to another location. You don't have to worry about remembering each and every link to your document. The Wizard does it for you.

To work with the Pack and Go Wizard:

1. Make sure that your Publisher document is complete and looks the way you want it to. Remember to save your work.

2. Select File⇨Pack and Go.

3. Pick one of two options:

- Use Take to Another Computer if you are sending the file to someone else or posting it on a Web server.

- Take to a Commercial Printing Service stores more formatting information that printers need to make sure that your document looks exactly the way you planned.

The Pack and Go Wizard opens. The first screen tells you what you can use the Wizard for.

4. Read the first screen and then click the Next button.

The second screen of the Wizard gives you the choice of where the packed files are saved. If you're physically carrying the file to another computer or to the printers, click A:\. This stores it to a floppy disk. If you're storing it on your own computer, or uploading it onto a server, use the Browse button to locate your desired directory destination.

5. After you've made your choice, click the Next button.

The third screen gives you the choice of what exactly is included in the packed file. If you're sending the file to a commercial printer, or to another computer that is not linked to yours by a server, make sure that all three check boxes are marked. If you're sending the file over an intranet, you can probably get away with just marking the Include Linked Graphics check box.

6. When you've made your selection, click the Next button.

The final screen of the Wizard basically recaps the parameters you've given it.

7. If everything is as you want it, click the Finish button.

The Wizard does the rest.

Personal Profiles

Publisher 2000 gives you the opportunity to create a personal profile to be inserted into the documents that you select. This can save a lot of time, precluding the need to input the information every time you create a new document. To do this:

1. Whenever you work through a Wizard from the Microsoft Publisher Catalog, the Personal Information dialog box appears. You can use this opportunity to fill out the information and include it in the document (if desired). Anytime you want to update your profile you can get to this dialog box by selecting Edit⇨Personal Information.

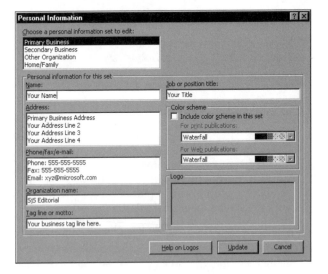

2. Publisher allows you to establish up to four profiles, one for each category of Primary Business, Secondary Business, Other Organization, and Home/Family. You can find these categories in the Choose a Personal Information Set to Edit window in the upper-left corner of the dialog box. Click the category you want to fill out.

3. Enter all the information requested in the dialog box. If there is a line of information that you don't want filled in, delete any text that appears in that line.

4. You can determine the color scheme associated with your personal information, and make it a different scheme for print publications than for Web publications. To do this, click the Include Color Scheme in This Set check box and then use the drop-down lists to select the colors for both print and Web publications.

5. You have the option of including a logo with your personal information. The logo appears in the box in the lower-right side of the dialog box.

6. When all the information is filled in, click the Update button.

   Publisher inserts this information in your documents according the parameters you establish for that document.

Publisher Wizards

Publisher 2000 provides you with professionally designed templates for over 100 different types of publications and has created a Wizard for each. It is possible to create a document without using the templates and the Wizards, but that is more work than you need and you should reserve that in the (extremely unlikely) event that Publisher doesn't have the template or style that you need.

To create a document using the Publisher Wizards:

1. Open Publisher.

   The first screen that appears is the Microsoft Publisher Catalog, which has three tabs, Publication, by Wizard, Publication, by Design, and Blank Publications.

   If you already have Publisher open and want to get to the Microsoft Publisher Catalog, you can do so by clicking File⇨New. For some reason, clicking the New button won't do it.

2. Make sure that the Publications by Wizard tab is on top.

   On the left side of the Publications by Wizard tab is a list of the available types of publications, with various style options displayed in the large window on the right side.

3. Click the type of publication you want to make.

   Some of the options have an arrow beside them, which indicates that they have several different variations for that type of publication. If the type of document you select has more than one template, click the style that most closely meets your needs.

4. When you've selected the type of publication you want to work with, the large window on the right demonstrates the different style options you can use. Scroll through the displays and select the style you want to use.

The exact same document templates appear in the Publications by Design tab as in the Publications by Wizard tab. The difference is that the Publications by Design tab allows you to search for a document template by design features and then by type of publication. If you know that you specifically want to work with one particular style (for example a floating oval master set design), you can use this tab to find all the document types that work with that style. When you do find the document template you want to use, the Wizard works exactly the same as if you found it through the Publications by Wizard tab.

5. Click the <u>S</u>tart Wizard button.

The first time you use the Wizard, you see a dialog box that prompts you to include your profile information. **See** "Personal Profiles" earlier in this section to know how to deal with this.

6. The first screen of the Wizard you've selected simply introduces you to the Wizard. Click the Next button to start the process.

7. The first choice of the Wizard allows you to determine the color scheme of your publication. If you click the various schemes, the window on the right displays how it will appear in the document. When you find the scheme you like the best, make sure it is highlighted and then click the Next button.

8. The next Wizard window you see depends on the type of document you've chosen. For example, the Quick Publications Wizard (which allows you to create simple, one-page documents) determines the layout of your document; the Newsletters Wizard gives you the option of determining how many columns exist on the page. After you've made your choice, click the Next button.

Multi-page publication styles have a nifty feature that appears in the center bottom part of your screen. It's a diagram of the different pages in the document style. Each page shows you a different design feature of the document style you're working with. Click the different pages to see how the different features work in your document.

9. From here on, the windows you see in the Wizard are totally dependent upon the type of document you're working with. Work through each screen, personalize your document the way you want, and click the Next button to move to further screens. If you want to change any decision you've already made, use the <u>B</u>ack button to return to previous screens.

10. When you've gotten to the last screen, click the Finish button.

A window opens with the familiar toolbar across the top, a document window on the right side, and a Wizard dialog box for the type of document on the left. You can use the Wizard dialog box to make changes to any of the decisions you've made in the opening windows of the wizard. Simply scroll down the window and click the options you want to change. A simplified version of the Wizard appears below it, where you can make any changes you want. You can make these changes at any time while you're working on the document.

 You see a Hide Wizard button on the bottom left side of the Publisher window. If you click this button, the Wizard disappears from your screen, giving you more room to work with the document. Don't worry; you can always get the Wizard back. After you've hidden the Wizard, the button changes to Show Wizard. Click it, and the Wizard returns, ready to do your bidding.

Text Frames

You can link different text frames together. You usually want to do this when the text you've inserted into one frame overflows to another. This can be handled automatically using Publisher's Autoflow feature (*see* "Autoflow"), or it can be done manually. Most of the time, I recommend using Autoflow; however, there are times when manually connecting text frames is a good idea. So here's how to do it:

1. Insert your text into the first text frame, as described in "Importing text from other applications."

If the text is too long for the frame, you see a dialog box that says "The inserted text doesn't fit in this frame. Do you want to use autoflow?" Click No.

At the bottom of the text frame, you see the Text in Overflow icon. This is merely there to alert you that you still have to find homes for the rest of the text.

2. Click the Connect Text Frames button or select Tools⇨ Connect Text Frames.

 Your cursor icon changes to a little pitcher (to catch the overflow).

3. Move to the text frame where you want to position the rest of the text. Click anywhere inside the frame.

Your extra text flows into that space.

 4. If you still have overflow, you can click the Connect Text Frame button again and move to a new text frame.

Notice that a little button appears at the bottom of the first text frame, at the top of the last text frame, and at both top and bottom of any text frames in the middle. Clicking this button moves you to either the previous frame containing the text (if at the top of the frame) or to the next frame (if at the bottom of the text).

5. Your next step is to have Publisher insert "Continued on..." messages at the end of each frame of the material. Move to the frame where the article or story starts, and click it.

6. Select Format⇨Text Frame Properties. The Text Frame Properties dialog box opens.

7. Click the Include "Continued on page..." check box.

8. If you want to, you can also click the Include "Continued from page..." check box as well.

9. Click OK.

Just as you can change the size of a text frame, you can add new ones to any document. To do this, simply:

 1. Click the Text Frame Tool button located on the Objects Toolbar.

2. Move your mouse to the point on your page where you want to put the new text frame.

3. Click once with the left mouse button.

4. The new text frame appears. At this time it is probably not the right size or shape for your needs. To adjust size and location of text frames, look at "Adjusting Text Frame Size," and "Moving a Text Frame to a different location," both in this part.

Part IX

Completing Complex Tasks

Welcome to the advanced class! The tasks described in this part are features of Office 2000 that go beyond the skills of the average user. You can use them to impress your boss and make your co-workers jealous. The great thing about all these tasks is that they work in most or all of the Office 2000 applications. Sure, some of them may look a little different in Word 2000 than they do in Publisher 2000, and they may even work a little differently between the two programs, but once you get the hang of it, you'll know how to use any of these tools in any program that supports them.

In this part . . .

✔ Creating hyperlinks to switch to associated files

✔ Embedding objects from one file to another application

✔ Writing macros to get your computer to do all the tedious chores

✔ Linking an object to another file

Embedding Objects in Your Documents

Embedding is the procedure where you take a section of one file in one application and make it a part of another. This is one application of the OLE technology that has been incorporated in the Office suites for a number of years. For example, you could take a chart from Excel 2000, or a table from Access 2000, or a graphic image, and embed it into a Word 2000 document. Or, you could take a body of text from Word and embed it into an Excel spreadsheet or into a PowerPoint frame.

The directions given in this section apply (with some cosmetic differences) to using the following applications as the destination file: Word 2000, Excel 2000, PowerPoint 2000, and in some instances into tables or queries of Access 2000. Publisher 2000 works a little differently; for information on how to embed (or link) objects into Publisher, please *see* Part VIII.

You need to know two special terms about embedding a file. These terms also apply for creating links and hyperlinks. A *source file* is the file from which you take the object to embed into the *destination file,* which is where that object will end up.

Generally, you want to embed only objects that are files of limited size (smaller than a single page). If you want to have access to the information in a larger file, I suggest you use a hyperlink instead. *See* "Hyperlinks" later in this part for information on this very useful tool.

Creating a new embedded object

Office 2000 lets you create a new embedded object into your destination file and then enter the data or text that fits your needs. Basically, what you're doing is creating an area where a different application (the source application) determines the appearance and formatting of the destination file. This is useful if you don't want to create a separate source file just to input information that you will only use in the destination file. For this set of steps, I am embedding an Excel chart into a Word document.

To create a new embedded object in a destination file:

1. Open the destination file and position the cursor at the point where you want the new object to be inserted.

2. Select Insert⇨Object from the menu bar.

The Object dialog box opens.

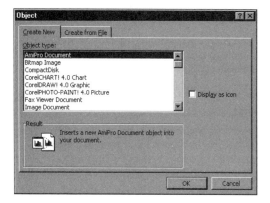

3. On the <u>C</u>reate New tab, scroll down the <u>O</u>bject type list until you find the application that you want to use for your embedded object (in this case, Microsoft Excel Chart). Highlight your selection and then click OK.

4. The object is inserted into your document.

At this point, the object contains placeholder information that you will need to edit to add your own information and particular style. This is covered in the next section, "Editing and formatting an embedded object."

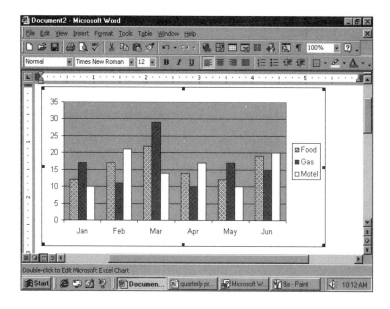

Editing and formatting an embedded object

After you have the object embedded in your destination document, you have to work with it a bit to make it fit your intent. It probably isn't the right shape or size, and it may not even display all the information you want it to. The following directions apply whether you've created a new object or have taken it from an existing source file.

1. Click anywhere inside the embedded object to select it. Then, right-click to see the pop-up menu.

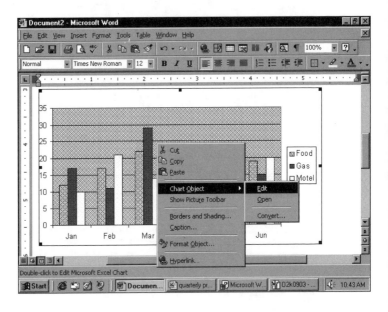

The name of the fourth item down on the pop-up menu changes depending on the source application. In the figure, it is called Chart Object; if I were working with a PowerPoint frame, it would be called a Presentation Object. In all cases, it contains the word "Object."

2. Click this item and select Edit.

The pop-up lists disappear and leave you looking at your unchanged embedded object. Don't despair; you didn't do anything wrong.

Right-click inside the object again. A new pop-up list appears. The appearance of this list differs according to the source application you're working with, but generally it has options to format the object, create a data source, determine the location of the information, and clear the object and start over.

Essentially what you're seeing at this point is a miniature version of the source application, but without the toolbars, and it allows you to do many of the same things the source application would.

3. Work through the items on this pop-up menu, using the techniques for the specific source destination as described in other parts of this book.

This pop-up menu reappears every time you right-click inside the object until you click outside its boundaries. You can, of course, go back and fiddle with the object at any time while you are working on the destination document; however, once an object is embedded, it is separate from the source file and changing one won't affect the other.

When you have the insides of the embedded object set the way you want, you now need to adjust its appearance to make it fit into the look of the rest of the destination file.

4. Choose View⇨Toolbars⇨Picture to open the Picture toolbar.

5. Use the buttons on the Picture toolbar to make the object the way you want it.

The Picture toolbar gives you nearly everything you need to make the object work with the rest of your document. The different Office applications have slightly different buttons on this toolbar. The table below gives you a brief description of the most common buttons on the toolbar and what they do.

Picture Toolbar Button	*Button Name*	*What It Does*
	Insert Picture	Allows you to insert a graphic file from your computer directory. When you click this button, an Insert Picture Navigator window opens. You can move through your system until you find the graphic you want to use and then click the Insert button.
	Image Control	This button gives you control over the colors of the embedded object. You have four choices: Automatic (which gives you the color settings that your computer is set to), Grayscale (which shows the object in black and white with shading done in gray), Black & White (just what it sounds like), and Watermark (the embedded object becomes faint and is suitable to be used as a background for other text or images).

(continued)

Picture Toolbar Button	Button Name	What It Does
	More Contrast	Allows you to increase the contrast between light and dark areas of the object. Generally, items that are printed in black and white need more contrast than items on a screen or those that are printed in color.
	Less Contrast	Allows you to reduce the contrast between the light and dark areas of the object. Contrast is most useful for graphic objects, less so for things like spreadsheets or bodies of text.
	More Brightness	Increases the apparent brightness of the object.
	Less Brightness	Decreases the apparent brightness of the object.
	Crop	Allows you to adjust the size of the object without changing the size of the items inside it. This is very useful for removing unwanted parts from the edges of an object and for making the object fit the space you have available. After this button is selected, your cursor shows the crop icon. If you click any selection handle (the little boxes around the frame of the object) you can then drag that side or corner inwards or outwards to adjust the size.
	Line Style	Shows a drop-down list with a number of different line styles that you can choose from for the border around your object.
	Text Wrapping	Gives you seven choices of text wrapping to control how close to the object the surrounding text appears.
	Format Object	This button opens a dialog box with six tabs that gives you control over the same features the other buttons on the Picture toolbar provide.
	Reset Picture	Returns the object to its original appearance.

Embedding a graphic object

One of the coolest things about embedding objects is that you can include pictures or drawings to liven up an otherwise tedious document. You *could* use the same technique as described in "Embedding an object from an existing file" to do this, but that's a lot more work than you need to do. Instead, try this:

1. Open the destination file and position your cursor where you want the object to go.

2. Select Insert⇨Picture from the menu bar.

A drop-down menu appears.

3. To import graphics, choose from either Clip Art or From File.

Choose Clip Art if you want to use one of the public domain images in the Microsoft Clip Gallery. Choose From File if you have a graphic image file of your own that you want to use.

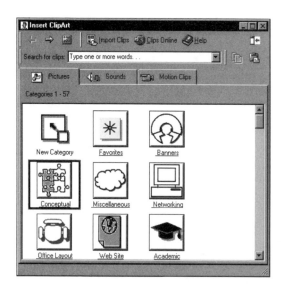

4. If you chose Clip Art, the Microsoft Clip Gallery opens.

The Clip Gallery gives you a selection of over 10,000 images to choose from. The first window you see gives you a group of images that act as a directory for similar images (usually grouped topically, but some — such as cartoons — are grouped stylistically). Click one of these images to see more images that match that grouping. When you find an image that you want to insert, click it to open a pop-up menu of four buttons. Click the Insert Clip button on the top of this menu. Your clip art selection is inserted into your document.

If you chose From File, an Explorer window opens and allows you to navigate through your computer system to find the file you want to use. When you find it, highlight it and click the Insert button at the bottom-right side of the window. Your image is now copied to the destination file.

5. When you have the image in your destination file, you can work with it to make it suit the needs of that particular document.

You do this the same as any other embedded object; *see* "Editing and formatting an embedded object" for information on how to do this.

Most graphic images can be formatted and edited like other embedded objects. However, bitmap images (files that have a .bmp extension) don't work the same. If you right-click inside an embedded bitmap object, and select Bitmap Image Object➪Edit, the toolbar from Microsoft Paint (included in both Windows 95 and 98) opens on the left side of your screen.

Embedding an object from an existing file

When you embed an object, it becomes a part of the file you've taken it to, but it retains its original formatting and appearance. When the object is embedded, you can fiddle with it in the new file without having to open the old application. Cool, huh? Here's how you do it:

1. Open the destination file and position the cursor at the point where you want the new object to be inserted.

2. Select Insert➪Object from the menu bar.

The Object dialog box opens.

3. Click the Create from File tab.

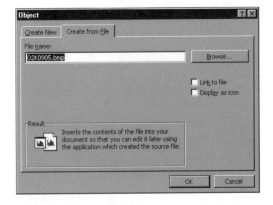

4. Click the Browse button to open a Browser window.

Navigate through your system until you find your desired source file.

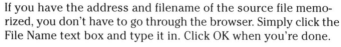

If you have the address and filename of the source file memorized, you don't have to go through the browser. Simply click the File Name text box and type it in. Click OK when you're done.

If you put a mark in the Link to File check box, the object appears on your screen just as with any other embedded object. However, it is actually *linked,* which means that the source file and the destination file have a connection. Any change that you make to the source file is automatically made in the destination file. However, the downside of this cool feature is that if you want to copy the destination file to another computer, you have to remember to copy the source file as well, otherwise the link won't work.

If you put a check in the Display as Icon check box on the Create from File dialog box, the object will appear in your document as an icon. If this happens, you won't see the actual embedded object until you print the destination document. The icons can't be modified or fiddled with in the destination file. If you want to play with the source file, you'll have to make sure that the Link to File box is checked and make all your changes in the source file. All in all, it's easier to keep Display as Icon blank and embed the actual file in your document.

5. When you find the source file, click the Insert button.

You return to the Create from File tab, and the filename appears in the text box.

6. Click OK.

The file is inserted into your document as an embedded object.

7. You will now probably want to fiddle with the embedded object to make it work with the destination file.

See "Editing and formatting an embedded object" for information on how to do this.

Hyperlinks

Hyperlinks are "hot spots" in an Office 2000 document that, when clicked, jump to a specific location within the current document, open another Office 2000 document, or display a page from the World Wide Web. By creating hyperlinks to other Office 2000 documents, you can effectively share information among documents without going to the trouble of using OLE or the Paste Link command. For example, a Word 2000 document that contains a marketing proposal may include a hyperlink to an Excel 2000 spreadsheet that contains all the specific figures.

People talk about source and destination files in both linking and embedding objects. Everyone uses the same terms with hyperlinks, but there is a significant difference that you need to understand. With linking and embedding objects, you are bringing another document (the source file) to the file we're working in (the destination file). Hyperlinks are the reverse. Hyperlinks are used to send the reader to someplace else (the destination file) from the document they started with (the source file). It's the difference between sending something someplace else (hyperlink) and bringing it to you (linking or embedding).

You can create a hyperlink in Word 2000, Excel 2000, PowerPoint 2000, Access 2000, FrontPage 2000 (but the process looks quite a bit different), or in the Web Page option of Publisher 2000. To create a hyperlink, simply follow these steps:

1. Open the source document (remember, your intent is to send someone to the destination). Highlight the text or object that you want to be the hyperlink.

This is the text that you want the user to click for the hyperlink.

2. Click the Insert Hyperlink button, or select Insert⇨Hyperlink.

An Insert Hyperlink dialog box appears.

3. If you did not highlight something in the source document before opening the dialog box, click the top text box, Text to Display, and type in the text that becomes the hyperlink in your source document. To the right of this text box is the ScreenTip button. If you click it, you get another dialog box that allows you to type in text that then appears in a small floating window whenever a cursor is positioned over the displayed hyperlink text.

4. Along the left side of the Insert Hyperlink dialog box are four buttons that allow you to control where the hyperlink actually goes. Each button opens a different dialog box that allows you to determine the destination of the hyperlink. Click one of the four options, as described here:

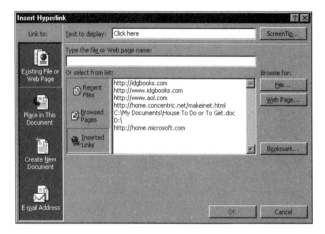

- The Existing File or Web Page button (shown in the previous figure) helps you locate other files or Web pages to be opened with the hyperlink. This only works with other files that your computer can reach (because they are on your hard drive), can be reached over an intranet, or can be found on the World Wide Web. You can browse for a File, a Web Page, or a Bookmark or select from a list of Recent Files, Browsed Pages, or other Inserted Links. When you find the file you want to send your reader to, highlight it and click OK.

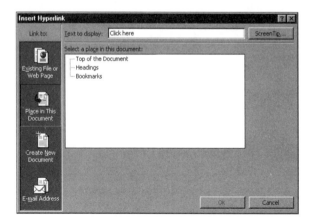

- The Place in This Document button sends the reader to another location in the same document to connect via the hyperlink. You may have to create a bookmark to get the hyperlink to go exactly where you want. Simply select the option that you want to send the reader to and click OK.

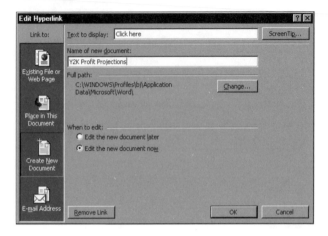

- The Create New Document button opens a new document window (of the same application you've been working with) that you can use to create a whole new destination document. Simply type in the filename for the new file, click Change to locate the directory where you want the destination file to go, and click OK. The new document opens before your eyes already linked to the source file.

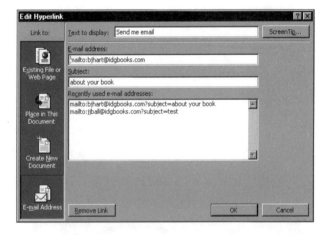

- The E-mail Address button opens a window that allows your reader to send e-mail to a particular e-mail address just by clicking the hyperlink. All you have to do is type in the e-mail address of the person you want the e-mail sent to, enter a subject line (though that is optional), and click OK. Whenever your reader clicks the hyperlink in the source document, Outlook opens a Send Mail window with the address already entered. Your readers can simply write whatever they want and click the Send button. Of course, this assumes that the reader uses Outlook Express for her e-mail. If she doesn't, then this hyperlink is of no use to her.

Links

Copying data from one program to another is easy enough, but what happens if you need to change the data? If you simply copy the data, you must track down every file to which you copied the data and update the data in each file. But if you *link* the data, any changes that you make to the original version of the data (the source file) automatically apply to copies of the linked data in the destination files.

Linking data is similar to embedding an object, except that a connection between the two files remains. If you send the destination file to another person, you need to send the source file as well, otherwise the link won't work.

Linking part of a file to another file

To copy data from one program to another and create a link, follow these steps:

1. Open the source file for the link.

2. Highlight the data that you want to copy by using the mouse or keyboard.

3. Press Ctrl+C, choose <u>E</u>dit⇨<u>C</u>opy, or click the Copy button, which appears on the Standard toolbar of all the Office 2000 programs.

4. Switch to the destination file.

5. Position the insertion point where you want to insert the data.

6. Choose <u>E</u>dit⇨Paste <u>S</u>pecial to summon the Paste Special dialog box, shown in this figure:

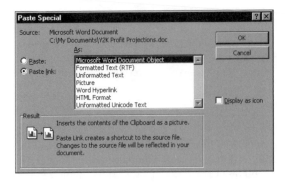

7. Click the Paste link radio button.

8. From the As text box, select how you want the link to be formatted in the destination file.

9. Click OK.

Whenever you open the file that contains the link, the program checks to see whether the data has changed. If so, it updates the link. That way, the data that appears in the document always reflects the most current version of the linked-to document.

Breaking a link

If you grow tired of the link and want to break it, follow this procedure:

1. Open the destination file for the link.

2. Choose Edit⇨Links.

The Links dialog box appears.

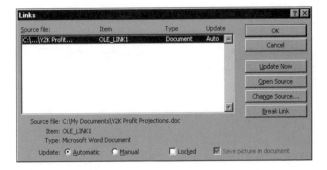

3. Select the link that you want to break from the Source file list.

4. Click the Break Link button.

5. When asked whether you really want to break the link, click the Yes button.

6. If links still remain in the document, you need to click OK to dismiss the Links dialog box. If you break the last link, the Links dialog box automatically vanishes.

The fastest way to remove a link from a destination file is to click on the object to select it and press the Delete key. The linked file will go away.

Macros

Macros enable you to record the commands you need to carry out common procedures. If you find yourself performing the same sequence of operations over and over again, you can often save a lot of time by recording these actions in a macro. Then, whenever you need to perform that repetitive task, all you need to do is click a button, and the macro performs the task for you. The following procedures apply to Word 2000, Excel 2000, and PowerPoint 2000. Access 2000 and support macros, too, but their macros are a bit more complicated and aren't covered in this book. The other Office 2000 programs do not support macros.

Recording a macro

To record a macro, follow these steps:

1. Think about what you're going to do and rehearse the procedure to make sure that you *really* know what you're doing.

2. Choose Tools⇨Macro⇨Record New Macro to open the Record Macro dialog box.

This dialog box varies just slightly between Word 2000, Excel 2000, and PowerPoint 2000. Here's how the Record Macro dialog box appears in Word 2000:

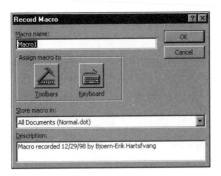

3. Type the name of your macro in the <u>M</u>acro name text box.

4. To make your macro accessible from a toolbar or the keyboard, click either the <u>T</u>oolbars or <u>K</u>eyboard button, assign the shortcut, and then click the Close button.

To help you assign the keyboard shortcut, a dialog box appears with a text box in which you can type the shortcut. Type the shortcut key you want to use, click the Assign button, and then click the Close button.

Note: The capability to assign the recorded macro to a keyboard shortcut while recording the macro is available *only* in Word 2000. To assign a macro to a keyboard shortcut in PowerPoint 2000 or Excel 2000, choose <u>T</u>ools➪<u>C</u>ustomize.

5. If you did not assign a keyboard shortcut in Step 4, click OK to begin recording the macro.

A little macro recorder toolbox appears, as shown here:

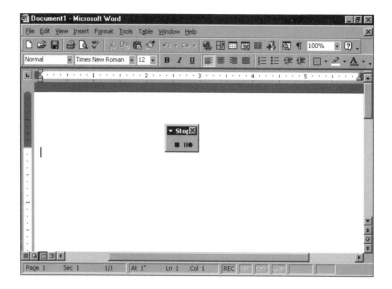

6. Type the keystrokes and menu commands that you want to record in the macro.

 Click the Pause Recording button in the macro toolbox if you need to temporarily suspend recording; click the Pause Recording button again to resume recording.

 7. After you finish recording, click the Stop Recording button.

You can now run the macro by using the procedure described in the following section, "Running a macro." If the macro doesn't work, you may have made a mistake while recording it. Record the macro again.

To delete a macro that you recorded incorrectly, choose Tools⇨Macro⇨Macros to open the Macros dialog box. Select the macro you want to delete and then click the Delete button to delete it.

Running a macro

Follow this procedure to run a macro you previously recorded:

1. Choose Tools⇨Macro⇨Macros to access the Macro dialog box.

2. Select the macro you want to run from the list of macros currently available.

3. Click the Run button.

Note: If you assigned a keyboard shortcut or toolbar button to the macro, you can run the macro by pressing the assigned keyboard shortcut or clicking the macro's button.

Sharing Data Between Programs

Access 2000 offers several features specially designed to share data with other Office 2000 applications. The following sections describe some of these features.

Merge It With Word

The Merge It With Word command provides an easy way to use Access 2000 data in a Word 2000 mail merge. Just follow these steps:

1. In Access 2000, open the database that contains the table that you want to use in a mail merge.

2. In the Main Switchboard, click Merge It With Word. The Microsoft Word Mail Merge Wizard dialog box appears.

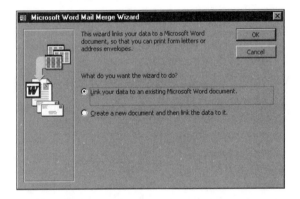

3. If the letter that you want to use for the mail merge already exists, click the Link your data to an existing Microsoft Word document, and then click the OK button.

4. An Explorer window opens, which allows you to select the document. When you find it, click the Open button again.

5. If you haven't yet created the document, click the <u>C</u>reate a new document button, and click OK.

Word opens to a new document that you can then use to write your letter (or whatever) with the address book information linked to it.

6. The new Word window opens with the Mail Merge toolbar specifically designed to help you create a merged document.

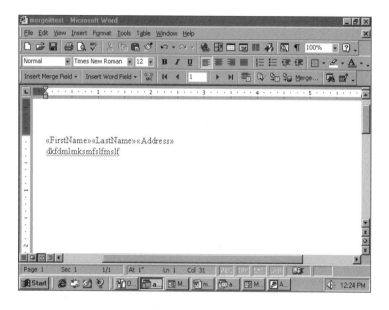

Some of the buttons on this toolbar are familiar to users of Access. However, there are some that might be new to you. The table below describes some of them:

Button	Name	Description
Insert Merge Field ▼	Insert Merge Field	Use this button to insert the data fields into the document at the cursor position. When you click this button, a drop-down list appears showing you all the available fields in the Access table.

(continued)

Button	*Name*	*Description*
Insert Word Field ▾	Insert Word Field	A really cool new feature. This button allows you to customize the text of the document according to the conditions that you establish. When you click this button, you see a drop-down list that allows you to establish the conditions and text that will change.
« » ABC	View Merged Data	Allows you to see your document with the data fields filled in by one of the records. Use the Record buttons to change which records you see. Great for checking that the Insert Word Field commands actually worked.
	Mail Merge Helper	Opens a dialog box that lets you create or edit a word document, the database, or the merge options.
	Check for Errors	Opens a dialog box that lets you tell your computer whether or not you want to be told about any errors that it finds in the document or in the merged fields.
	Merge to New Document	Creates a new Word document with the merge fields of the displayed record inserted. This is not a merged document, it has the information of only a single record in it.
	Merge to Printer	Opens your Printer dialog box. Use this when you're ready to print out your letters.
Merge...	Start Mail Merge	Opens the Merge dialog box, which lets you determine which records are inserted into the merged document. Useful if you don't want all the records in your database to be merged with the document.

Button	Name	Description
	Find Record	Opens a dialog box that lets you locate a specific record based upon the criteria you select. For example, if you want to find the record of Lee Johnson, you could select "Johnson" in the "LastName" field.
	Edit Data Source	Opens the database table so that you can enter or change any information you need.

Publish It

You can convert an Access 2000 table, query, form, or report to a Word 2000 table by using the Publish It With MSWord command. Here is the procedure:

1. In Access 2000, open the database that contains the database object that you want to convert to a Word 2000 document.

2. Select the database object (a table, query, form, or report) that you want to convert.

3. Choose Tools⇨OfficeLinks⇨Publish It With MSWord.

4. Watch as Access 2000 converts the data to a Word 2000 document.

Write-Up

PowerPoint 2000 includes a feature called Write-Up that lets you convert a presentation to Word 2000 format. Here's how to use the new Write-Up feature:

1. In PowerPoint 2000, open the presentation that you want to convert.

2. Choose File⇨Send To⇨Microsoft Word.

The Write-Up dialog box appears, as shown in the following figure:

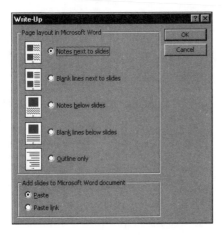

3. Write-Up provides several options for how you want to format the presentation in Word 2000, as indicated by the sample document styles shown next to the radio buttons. Choose the formatting option you want by clicking its radio button.

The Paste and Paste Link options determine whether a link should be established between the original PowerPoint 2000 presentation and the converted Word 2000 document. If you select the Paste option, no link is established. If you specify Paste Link, a link is created so that whenever the slides in the original PowerPoint 2000 presentation change, the corresponding information in the converted Word 2000 document change as well.

4. Click OK and then wait while Write-Up launches Word 2000 and converts your presentation.

This may take a few moments, but eventually the presentation appears in Word 2000 as an open document.

5. Choose File⇨Save if you want to save the converted file.

Index

G

H

I

J

K

Dummies Books™
Bestsellers on Every Topic!

Dummies Books™
Bestsellers on Every Topic!

TECHNOLOGY TITLES

SUITES

Microsoft® Office 2000 For Windows® For Dummies®	Wallace Wang & Roger C. Parker	0-7645-0452-5	$19.99 US/$28
Microsoft® Office 2000 For Windows® For Dummies®, Quick Reference	Doug Lowe & Bjoern Hartsfvang	0-7645-0453-3	$12.99 US/$19
Microsoft® Office 98 For Macs® For Dummies®	Tom Negrino	0-7645-0229-8	$19.99 US/$28

WORD PROCESSING

Word 2000 For Windows® For Dummies®, Quick Reference	Peter Wererlet	0-7645-0449-5	$12.99 US/$19
Word 97 For Windows® For Dummies®	Dan Gookin	0-7645-0052-X	$19.99 US/$26
WordPerfect® 7 For Windows® 95 For Dummies®	Margaret Levine Young & David Kay	1-56884-949-4	$19.99 US/$26

SPREADSHEET/FINANCE/PROJECT MANAGEMENT

Excel 2000 For Windows® For Dummies®	Greg Harvey	0-7645-0446-0	$19.99 US/$28
Excel 2000 For Windows® For Dummies® Quick Reference	John Walkenbach	0-7645-0447-9	$12.99 US/$19
Microsoft® Money 99 For Dummies®	Peter Weverka	0-7645-0433-9	$19.99 US/$28
Microsoft® Project 98 For Dummies®	Martin Doucette	0-7645-0321-9	$24.99 US/$34

WEB DESIGN & PUBLISHING

Creating Web Pages For Dummies®, 4th Edition	Bud Smith & Arthur Bebak	0-7645-0504-1	$24.99 US/$34
FrontPage® 98 For Dummies®	Asha Dornfest	0-7645-0270-0	$24.99 US/$34
HTML 4 For Dummies®	Ed Tittel & Stephen Nelson James	0-7645-0331-6	$29.99 US/$42
Java™ For Dummies®, 2nd Edition	Aaron E. Walsh	0-7645-0140-2	$24.99 US/$34

MACINTOSH

Macs® For Dummies®, 6th Edition	David Pogue	0-7645-0398-7	$19.99 US/$28
Macs® For Teachers™, 3rd Edition	Michelle Robinette	0-7645-0226-3	$24.99 US/$34
The iMac For Dummies	David Pogue	0-7645-0495-9	$19.99 US/$26

NETWORKING

Building An Intranet For Dummies®	John Fronckowiak	0-7645-0276-X	$29.99 US/$42
Client/Server Computing For Dummies®, 2nd Edition	Doug Lowe	0-7645-0066-X	$24.99 US/$34
Lotus Notes® Release 4 For Dummies®	Stephen Londergan & Pat Freeland	1-56884-934-6	$19.99 US/$26
Networking For Dummies®, 4th Edition	Doug Lowe	0-7645-0498-3	$19.99 US/$28
Upgrading & Fixing Networks For Dummies®	Bill Camarda	0-7645-0347-2	$29.99 US/$42

GENERAL INTEREST TITLES

BUSINESS & PERSONAL FINANCE

Accounting For Dummies®	John A. Tracy, CPA	0-7645-5014-4	$19.99 US/$26
Business Plans For Dummies®	Paul Tiffany, Ph.D. & Steven D. Peterson, Ph.D.	1-56884-868-4	$19.99 US/$26
Home Buying For Dummies®	Eric Tyson, MBA & Ray Brown	1-56884-385-2	$16.99 US/$24
Investing For Dummies®	Eric Tyson, MBA	1-56884-393-3	$19.99 US/$26
Marketing For Dummies®	Alexander Hiam	1-56884-699-1	$19.99 US/$26
Mutual Funds For Dummies®, 2nd Edition	Eric Tyson, MBA	0-7645-5112-4	$19.99 US/$26
Personal Finance For Dummies®, 2nd Edition	Eric Tyson, MBA	0-7645-5013-6	$19.99 US/$26
Selling For Dummies®	Tom Hopkins	1-56884-389-5	$16.99 US/$24
Successful Presentations For Dummies®	Malcolm Kushner	1-56884-392-5	$16.99 US/$24
Time Management For Dummies®	Jeffrey J. Mayer	1-56884-360-7	$16.99 US/$24

THE ARTS

Blues For Dummies®	Lonnie Brooks, Cub Koda, & Wayne Baker Brooks	0-7645-5080-2	$24.99 US/$34
Classical Music For Dummies®	David Pogue & Scott Speck	0-7645-5009-8	$24.99 US/$34
...z For Dummies®	Dirk Sutro	0-7645-5081-0	$24.99 US/$34
...no For Dummies®	Blake Neely of Cherry Lane Music	0-7645-5105-1	$24.99 US/$34

*For more information, or to order,
call (800)762-2974*

Discover Dummies™ Online!

The *Dummies* Web Site is your fun and friendly online resource for the latest information about *...For Dummies®* books on all your favorite topics. From cars to computers, wine to Windows, and investing to the Internet, we've got a shelf full of *...For Dummies* books waiting for you!

Ten Fun and Useful Things You Can Do at www.dummies.com

1. Register this book and win!
2. Find and buy the *...For Dummies* books you want online.
3. Get ten great *Dummies Tips™* every week.
4. Chat with your favorite *...For Dummies* authors.
5. Subscribe free to *The Dummies Dispatch™* newsletter.
6. Enter our sweepstakes and win cool stuff.
7. Send a free cartoon postcard to a friend.
8. Download free software.
9. Sample a book before you buy.
10. Talk to us. Make comments, ask questions, and get answers!

Jump online to these ten fun and useful things at
http://www.dummies.com/10useful

For other technology titles from IDG Books Worldwide, go to
www.idgbooks.com

Not online yet? It's easy to get started with *The Internet For Dummies®,* 5th Edition, or *Dummies 101®: The Internet For Windows® 98,* available at local retailers everywhere.

Find other *...For Dummies* books on these topics:

Business • Careers • Databases • Food & Beverages • Games • Gardening • Graphics
Hardware • Health & Fitness • Internet and the World Wide Web • Networking • Office Suites
Operating Systems • Personal Finance • Pets • Programming • Recreation • Sports
Spreadsheets • Teacher Resources • Test Prep • Word Processing

IDG BOOKS WORLDWIDE BOOK REGISTRATION

Register
This Book
and Win!

We want to hear from you!

Visit **http://my2cents.dummies.com** to register this book and tell us how you liked it!

- ✔ Get entered in our monthly prize giveaway.

- ✔ Give us feedback about this book — tell us what you like best, what you like least, or maybe what you'd like to ask the author and us to change!

- ✔ Let us know any other *...For Dummies*® topics that interest you.

Your feedback helps us determine what books to publish, tells us what coverage to add as we revise our books, and lets us know whether we're meeting your needs as a *...For Dummies* reader. You're our most valuable resource, and what you have to say is important to us!

Not on the Web yet? It's easy to get started with *Dummies 101*®: *The Internet For Windows*® *98* or *The Internet For Dummies*®, 5th Edition, at local retailers everywhere.

Or let us know what you think by sending us a letter at the following address:

...For Dummies Book Registration
Dummies Press
7260 Shadeland Station, Suite 100
Indianapolis, IN 46256-3917
Fax 317-596-5498

BESTSELLING
BOOK SERIES